L.M.S. MISCELLANY

A Pictorial Record of the Company's Activities
in the Public Eye and Behind the Scenes

Volume Three

H. N. Twells

Volume One produced 1982
Volume Two produced 1984

Oxford Publishing Company

Acknowledgements

I would once again like to warmly thank a number of friends for the loan of photographs and other LMS material during the preparation of this third volume of *LMS Miscellany*. Without their assistance, the task of compiling a volume of this nature would be more difficult.

My thanks are therefore due to Roy Anderson, Mike Brooks, Tom Collinge, Gordon Coltas, H. C. Casserley, Mike Christenson, John Edgington, Vic Forster, Glenn Foxley, John Hinchliffe, Dr Jack Hollick, David Jenkinson, David Ibbotson, Jim Kay, Lawrence Knighton, Barry Lane, John Miller, George Norman, Mike Peascod, Brian Radford, Don Rowland, Bill Stubbs (for his own prints and from the W. L. Good and L. Hanson collections) Peter Tatlow, Stuart Underwood, Glyn Waite, Graham Warburton, Norman Williams, and the staff at the Post Office Museum, and the National Railway Museum.

If I have omitted anyone, then my sincere apologies and thanks go to them.

The quest for fresh LMS material will continue, and if anyone has further information, photographs or other material from the LMS, then they are invited to write to me at the Publisher's address, as such information and material could be useful for further volumes on the LMS. In this respect, the next book will cover the LMS contribution to the World War II effort. The LMS was a vast organisation and it still captivates the interest of so many.

Finally, my warmest thanks go to my family, for putting up with the constant patter of the typewriter, and the disarray which inevitably results from spreading material around the home.

LMS Miscellany Volume II — amendments and additional information.

Plate 238 — Believed to be at the south end of Crewe rather than the north end, and the train was a test train, to test the performance of electric motor bogies at high speeds.

Plate 24 — The Rushworth excursion from Liverpool (Lime Street) ran every year prior to the 1939 outbreak of war to the Radiolympia Exhibition, for staff and customers.

Plate 45 — A photograph taken at Ballymena, not Belfast, and the wagons in the background are narrow gauge hopper wagons used for bringing iron ore down from Cargan and Parkmore to Ballymena.

Plate 239 — What appears to be a 'staged' derailment was in fact an actual occurrence. I am advised that a broken rail joint was the cause, and rerailing was achieved by using jacks and slewing the bogie over the rail. My informant reports having stood alongside the photographer when the photograph was taken.

British Library Cataloguing in Publication Data

Twells, H.N.
  L.M.S. miscellany: a pictorial record
  of the company's activities in the
  public eye and behind the scenes.
  Vol.3
  1. London, Midland and Scottish Railway
  —History — Pictorial works.
  I. Title
  385'.0941   HE3020.LY5

Typesetting by:
Colin Powell Typesetting & Design, St. Michaels Road, Bournemouth, Dorset.

Printed in Great Britain by:
Netherwood Dalton & Co. Ltd., Huddersfield, Yorks.

Published by:
Oxford Publishing Co.
Link House
West Street
POOLE, Dorset

Index of Contents by Plate Number

	Plates
The Directors and LMS Board Room	1–6
LMS 1926 Strike Medal	7
Euston House	8
Tunnels on the LMS	9–19
Catering	21–22
Playing Cards	23–24
LMS Magazine & Staff Publications	25–31
LMS Stone Quarrying	35–38
Preservation	39, 67, 68
Locomotives Nos. 1–11111	40–43
Snow Hazard	44–48
Sleet Vans	49–51
Automatic 'Stone' Signals	52–53
Toton Marshalling Yards and Shed	54–60
Coal traffic Handling	61–65
Uniforms	69
Wages Paid	70–71
Trackwork Contractors	73–76
Training Motor Drivers	77–78
'Insets' Advertising Tickets	83–84
Railway Servants Orphanages	85–86
Triumph of the 'Royal Scot'	88–98
The LMS in North America	99–100
Passenger Station Detail	101–120
Land Ownership	121–124
Cigarette Cards	125
LMS Divers	126–127
LMS Launderies	128–129

	Plates
Carriage Pictures	130–131
The West Coast Road Route	132
Gleneagles Hotel	133–135
Gradients on the LMS	136–144
British Empire Exhibition, Wembley	145, 148
LMS Employees	149–156
LMS Research Laboratory, Derby	157
Unusual Motive Power	158–164
Travelling Post Offices	166–176
LMS Internal Letter Sorting Arrangements	177
Ambulance Team	178
Diesel Locomotives used by the LMS	179–187
General Traffic	188–202
Executive Research Office	203–206
Barrows and Trolleys	207–215
Insurance Tickets	222
Prewar Engine Postcards	231
Single Line Working	232–234
Double-headed Trains	235–249
LMS Films and Cinema Coach	250–251
Push-Pull	252–253
Freight by Road	254–257
Stationary Boilers	258–260
The 'Coronation Scot'	262–263
LMS Finale	264–265
Miscellaneous Items	32–34, 66, 72, 79, 80–82, 87, 146–7, 165, 216–221, 223–230, 261

The contents of LMS Miscellany Volumes I & II are listed on the final page of this volume, thus giving a complete summary of this title.

Introduction

This third volume consisting of 265 LMS photographs is presented as a further selection of photographs to add to the 246 in *LMS Miscellany (Volume I)* and 243 in *(Volume II)*, illustrating the many diverse aspects of this once great railway company. I hope that it will be seen, with the two previous volumes, as a source of information and interest which was not previously readily available to the railway enthusiast. The modeller too should find an abundance of information which will be of interest in the quest for prototype accuracy in whatever scale he should select to operate.

It would, however, be wrong to assume that the contents of these three volumes represent a fully comprehensive story of the London, Midland & Scottish Railway Company. Aspects such as architecture, signalling, carriage & wagon matters, locomotives and liveries, have all been covered by fellow members of the LMS Society with books published by the publisher of this volume, Oxford Railway Publishing Company. In addition, other publishers and authors have covered matters such as motive power depots. My hope is that the three volumes will live alongside these other specialist subjects to provide a lasting account of the Company's activities behind the scenes, and those aspects which for the most part, the public would not normally have been aware of.

There are still some aspects, however, which have not found space within this volume, and there is always the chance that further new information and material will become available from further research being undertaken.

During the preparation of this volume there were one or two points which I thought would fit into the introduction as examples of the way the LMS was concerned with detail. In April 1932, the Company proposed that a number of vehicles in the 'Royal Scot' train formations should be wired to receive wireless broadcasts whilst en route. Headphones would be provided for passengers at a charge of 1/-, and they estimated that revenue would be approximately £1 per day. The experiment was agreed for a trial period of six months, with the outlay for headphone sets of £1,228. Difficulties in reception of programmes led to the withdrawal of this service, with the cause identified as the steel carriages causing interference with the broadcast signals. The headphones were returned to the manufacturer and the LMS received a full refund of the cost of the equipment. In February 1933, a proposal was made for trade advertising on the 'Smoking' and 'Smoking Prohibited' stickers on carriage windows. The stickers were to be supplied to the Company free of charge and net revenue was estimated to reach £1,000 in the first and second years, and double, to £2,000 in the third and subsequent years. The scheme was agreed for six months, and the prohibited sticker was to be changed to 'Non-Smoking'. To what extent advertising was done in this way is not stated in official records.

Many of the modernisation schemes and alterations to company installations were approved under the Government Loan Guarantee Schemes available at the time, and this enabled the Company to link into finance for approved capital projects which was available at reduced rates of interest for periods of up to five years. A rate of 5 per cent applied in 1931, and no doubt the rate varied in line with budget and fiscal policy, much as it does today, although once the finance was drawn, the rate would remain constant.

Such was the importance of the proposal to replace the metal 'pots de chambre' in the LMS sleeping cars with porcelain 'recepticals', that it was referred to the main Board of Directors in March 1931 for a decision, and approval subsequently given.

These are but a few of the many small points to have come out of my researches.

In previous volumes, I have used small adverts from the LMS public timetables and LMS ticket issues to add interest to the photographic content. By way of further variation, a selection of the cast plates fitted by the Company to rolling stock, to bridges and other installations, together with a selection of luggage labels which in themselves represent many different styles, and small items of paperwork, have been used in this volume. Most will have an obvious purpose, but the LMS horse-brass alongside *Plate 211*, and the Wolverton 1938 plate beneath *Plate 215*, typical of those fitted to all the Company's horse-drawn vehicles, are less obvious examples.

It is always of interest to receive letters from those who have read a particular work, and after the publication of the second volume, a gentleman wrote to say he had had 48 years service, first with the L&NWR, the LMS, and then British Railways, and he had enjoyed the book. His general comments were appreciative, and he had been pleased to see the photographs of the Rhyl LMS Male Voice Choir — *Plates 1 & 2* — and particularly that his father, who had been one of the choir founders was on both photographs. The same gentleman had worked as part of the team clearing up bomb-damaged St. Pancras Station shown in *Plates 104 & 105*, and for him the book had rekindled many past memories. He is one of those who from their own experience, can still throw much light on the operational side of the LMS. Thank you, Alf Sibley, and thanks too to the many other people who have taken the trouble to write and express their appreciation. It is a great encouragement to know that my original aim of providing a selection of photographs of the LMS 'behind the scenes' may have been fulfilled and has been of interest to so many.

H. N. Twells
Chesterfield,
1986

Plate 1: Lord Stamp of Shortlands, Chairman and President of the Executive.
Author's Collection

The Directors

Not surprisingly, the Company's Directors came from the pre-group companies, with the honour of being first Chairman of the new London, Midland & Scottish Railway Company falling to the Chairman of the London & North Western Railway Company, Lord Lawrence of Kingsgate. Sir Guy Granet, GBE, former Chairman of the Midland Railway, and Mr E. B. Fielden, JP, the last Chairman of the Lancashire & Yorkshire Railway Company, became Deputy Chairmen.

Lord Lawrence resigned as Chairman at the Company's First Annual General Meeting held at Euston on 29th February 1924, and was succeeded by Sir Guy Granet. From a gross receipts figure of £91 million, a surplus over expenditure of £19.9 million was achieved, and this led directly to calls for reductions in the freight rates charged, which were implemented later that year. A first successful year for the largest railway company in the world.

Sir Josiah C. Stamp, GBE, joined the Board in December 1925 as the First President of the Executive, and his name is perhaps the one which, more than any other Director, is most closely associated with the development of the LMS Company. He succeeded Sir Guy Granet as Chairman in the autumn of 1927, and remained at the head of the Company until his untimely death at the age of 61, through enemy action, on 17th April 1941. In the 1938 Birthday Honours List, His Majesty King George VI conferred a Baronetcy on Sir Josiah, and he took the title, Lord Stamp of Shortlands.

There were many changes on the Board during the Company's 25 year period and many eminent personalities served the Company. Directors were issued with all-line gold passes for first class travel, and one of their many duties was to join the tours to various parts of the system, which were arranged at intervals. There were many responsibilities, and these included attendance at ceremonies and staff functions, where individual achievements were recognised through the award of trophies.

In addition to the main Board of Directors, there was a Northern Board, which took responsibility for operations in the Northern Division — north of Carlisle.

Directors were also required to serve on the various Joint Committees and connected operations, which included the following principal committees:

Aberdeen Joint Station
Axholme Joint Railway
Belfast & North Counties
Birmingham Canal Navigations
Caledonian & North British Railways (1908) Agreement
Carlingford Lough Commission
Carlisle (Dentonholme) Station
Cheshire Lines
County Donegal Railway Board
Dee Conservancy Board
Dublin & South Eastern Board
Dumbarton & Balloch Joint Line
Dundalk, Newry & Greenore Board
Dundee & Arbroath Joint Line
Forth Bridge Board
Girvan Harbour Commission
Grangemouth Branch Railway
Great Central Committees previously with the L&NWR: the Midland:
North Staffordshire Railway: Hull & Barnsley & Midland:
Great Northern Committees with the L&NWR & Midland
Great Northern Joint Stations
Great Western Joint Committees with the L&NWR: the Midland: Brecon & Merthyr: Rhymney:
Halifax & Ovenden Joint
Halifax High Level Joint
Humber Conservancy Board
Leeds New Station Joint
Maryport Harbour Commission
Methley Railway Board
Norfolk & Suffolk Joint Railways

Normanton Station Committee
Oldham, Ashton & Guide Bridge Board
Otley & Ilkley Joint Line
Pension Fund (L&YR)
Perth General Station
Perth Station Hotel
Princes Dock Branch Railway
Railway Clearing House (Irish)
The Railway Clearing House
Railway Companies Association
Somerset & Dorset Board
Somerset & Dorset Joint Committee
South Yorkshire Joint Line
Strabane & Letterkenny Railway Board
Superannuation Fund Boards for the former, L&NWR, Midland, Caledonian and Lancashire & Yorkshire
Swinton & Knottingley Joint
Tebay Joint Station
Tottenham & Hampstead Joint
Upper Mersey Navigation Commission
Wakefield Westgate Joint Station
West London Extension Board
Whitechapel & Bow Board
Whitechapel & Bow Joint Committee
Widows & Orphans
Railway Air Services Ltd.
Huddersfield Joint Omnibus Committee
Halifax Joint Omnibus Committee
Todmorden Joint Omnibus Committee
Sheffield Joint Omnibus Committee

By 1st January 1937 — a point close to the mid-point in the Company's existence — the organisation was as follows:

Chairman of the Board and President of the Executive Committee.

4 Vice-Presidents, Chief Legal Adviser, Secretary of the Company, Chief Executive Officer for New Works & Parliamentary Business, and the Executive, formed the Executive Committee.

Vice-President (1) responsible for: Executive Research Office

Vice-President (2) responsible for: Railway Traffic Operating & Commercial Section (Traffic, Operating, Passenger & Commercial)

Departments:
  Chief Operating Manager,
  Chief Commercial Manager,
  Chief Officer for Scotland
  Estate Manager

Vice-President (3) responsible for: Works & Ancilliary Undertakings & Director of Scientific Research

Departments:
  Chief Civil Engineer,
  Chief Mechanical Engineer,
  Signal & Telegraph Engineer,
  Electrical Engineer,
  Road Motor Engineer,
  Chief Marine Superintendent,
  Research Manager

Vice-President (4) responsible for: Finance & Service Departments

Departments
  Secretary's & Registrar's and Savings Bank
  Solicitor
  Chief Accountant
  Chief Stores Superintendent
  Rating Agent
  Chief Office for Labour & Establishment

The Controller, LMS Hotel Services, came under the direct supervision of the President of the Executive.

  Much of the Chief Operating Manager's and Chief Commercial Manager's Departments were intertwined for operational expediency.

  Within these various Departments there were senior officers with specific responsibilities covering every aspect of the Company's vast array of services.

Plate 2: The Board Room at Euston in June, 1946. The clock still carries the L&NWR initials.

British Railways

Plate 3: The cover and opening pages of the Director's pocketbook.
M. Peascod Collection

The days, hours and places given in the Calendar are those of the Meetings when held in ordinary course; they are, however, subject to alteration, of which due notice will be given.

PRIVATE.

Roll of Directors

AND

OFFICERS OF THE COMPANY,

STATISTICS AND DATES OF MEETINGS.

MARCH, 1923, to MARCH, 1924.

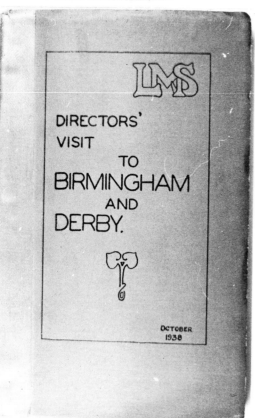

Plate 4: The Directors visited installations in Birmingham & Derby on the 4th & 5th October 1938, and a typescript with photographs formed an illustrated handbook for the visit; the cover is shown in this photograph. The Directors' Saloon was attached to the 9.15a.m. Euston to Birmingham train arriving at 11.10a.m. Local transport was provided for a visit to the Road Motor Engineer's Workshops at Saltley, prior to lunch at 1p.m. at the Queens Hotel, a Company hostelry. The Directors' Saloon was attached to the 2.10p.m. Birmingham to Derby train, arriving at 3.12p.m., and cars conveyed the Directors to the School of Transport, and later to the Research Laboratory. The night was spent at the Midland Hotel. The morning was taken up with a visit to the Carriage & Wagon Works, followed by lunch at the Midland Hotel. The Locomotive Works and the Company's power-station were the attraction after lunch, before the Directors' Saloon was attached to the 3.36p.m. Derby to St. Pancras express to conclude the tour.

Author's Collection

Plate 5 (above right): The Electrical sub-station building in the Locomotive Works, one of the attractions for the Directors' visit.

Author's Collection

Plate 6: Directors' Saloon No. 2552 at Halesowen Junction in May 1930. This was originally built by the Midland Railway as a 6-wheel inspection saloon in 1887, and rebuilt as a bogie saloon in 1908.

W. L. Good

Plate 7: The medal and case — the **Latin inscription has LMSR as the first** letter of the left-hand column. The statue's arms are outstretched with a locomotive supported by each arm. The reverse lettering reads — For Service National Emergency May 1926. There is no doubt that the Company understood the threat and acknowledged the loyalty of their employees that year, both to the **Company and the country.**

S. G. Underwood Collection

EUSTON STATION.

January, 1927.

Dear Sir,

 With reference to the previous communication to you, I have now the pleasure to send, for your acceptance, the medal which has been struck by the Company to commemorate the success of the loyal citizens of the Country in their resistance to the menace to the Constitution in May last.

 The inscription on the reverse of the medal incorporating the initials L.M.S.R. seems to express happily the spirit of the people, and I translate it to mean that Generosity of Service is the Salvation of the Commonwealth.

 I regret that I have not been able to forward the medal earlier, but I hope you will agree that the excellence of the design justifies the time spent in its preparation and execution.

Yours faithfully,

President of the Executive.

C. Stonier, Esq.

EUSTON HOUSE

Plate 8: Euston House, the Company's modern offices, opened on 12th February 1934, only eleven months after the builders were given the go-ahead. This 9-storey building housed the London District Passenger Manager's staff, the Commercial, Operating, Signal & Telegraph and Stores Departments. Air-conditioning ensured a change of air every 20 minutes, and there were 600 radiators having a capacity of 10,000 gallons of hot water. It is perhaps surprising that Portland stone and bricks were used, to the exclusion of the Company's own stone supplies at the Caldon Low quarries in Staffordshire. Some 1,300 employees could be accommodated in this building, and four passenger high-speed lifts were provided. A cinema was attached to the photographic unit, to enable the Company to show its services on film to interested industrial and commercial customers. One innovative feature was a waste-paper chute, with reception points on each floor, which allowed all scrap paper to be deposited direct into a central tip in the basement, adjoining which was a baling machine for compressing the waste, and packing it ready for disposal. More than 50 years after opening, it is still in use by British Railways today.

Author's Collection

TUNNELS ON THE LMS

Totley Tunnel on the LMS Hope Valley route, between Sheffield and Manchester, was the second longest tunnel in Great Britain, with a bore 3 miles 950yds. long, straight, but for the last 80yds. or so at the Grindleford end. The GWR claimed the longest with the Severn Tunnel, 4 miles 636yds. in length.

There were a further 26 tunnels on LMS routes which exceeded one mile in length, and quite a number between 30yds. and one mile — approximately 150 on the Midland Division alone.

Railway tunnels were not the only ones owned by the Company, for there were canal tunnels also, the most notable being the 'Standedge' narrow tunnel which the L&NWR had taken over in 1847 when it acquired the Huddersfield & Manchester Railway Company. It had owned the canal and two rail bores.

The canal tunnel was 3 miles 135yds. long when first built, and could claim the unique distinction of being the highest canal in Great Britain, 648ft. above sea level, and to traverse the Pennines from Huddersfield to Ashton, near Manchester, required passage through 42 locks in 8 miles ascending 438ft. 10in. on the east side, and 32 locks in 9 miles descending through 338ft. on the western side of the mountains.

The canal tunnel was one of four bores at Standedge, there being two single line and the new double line tunnel added in 1894. All four bores were linked with ventilation airways and shafts. Standedge was but one of the locations.

Tunnel excavations were hazardous and time-consuming, and progress relied on considerable numbers of men being available, aided by horses and small gauge railway tracks for the spoils to be taken away.

As the railway network developed and the early lines required widening to cope with the rapidly increasing traffic around the turn of the century, new tunnel bores were made, and on the stretch of line between St. Pancras and Chesterfield, there were 'twin' tunnels in nine locations. In some locations, tunnels were excavated and opened out into deep cuttings, and there are illustrations in *LMS Miscellany (Volume I)* — *Plate 62,* and *LMS Miscellany (Volume II)* — *Plates 186 & 187.* At Sharnbrook, on the Midland main line, the goods tunnel was excavated at a lower level than the main line to avoid the heavy grades to the summit at this point.

The oldest railway tunnel was the 'Glenfield' Tunnel, opened in 1832 by the Leicester & Swannington Railway, and this was probably the oldest railway tunnel in the world. It was virtually level and straight throughout, and when the first train with passengers passed through, legend has it that the chimney of the engine became lodged and this caused a great deal of discomfort to the passengers and guests who were on the train for the opening of the line. The Glenfield tunnel remained open throughout the LMS period.

Totley Tunnel was straight, but for a short section at the western end, but part-way through, there was a summit and level stretch, with gradients up from each entrance. Eight platelayers' cabins are located in the tunnel, each with cooking and ablution facilities, and stretcher and first-aid equipment, seven on the north wall, the one on the opposite side having initially been equipped as an underground signal cabin. There were two seven-man gangs of permanent way men looking after maintenance under the control of a permanent way Inspector.

Tunnel inspections were carried out every six months using specially equipped vans and powerful electric searchlights, and it is recorded that on one occasion when the tunnel was 'swept', eight wagons of soot were brought out.

In the longer tunnels, alarm wires were carried through the bore about 6ft. above ground level, and in the event of one of these being severed in an emergency, alarm bells would be rung in the signal boxes at either end of the tunnel.

Totley Tunnel was a particularly wet one, and the water was collected in a drainage culvert which maintained a supply of water to the engine sheds at Millhouses and Grimesthorpe, and the respective stations also.

Many other tunnels could be mentioned for some pecularity or special point of interest, such as the short-equilibrium tunnel (axis-tilted for unequal loading) between the two original High Tor Tunnels at Matlock, to deflect any large rock fall from the nearby High Tor; the little Toadmoor Tunnel at Ambergate, an ellipse in section with long axis horizontal for lateral pressure; Spital Tunnel, Sheffield, for exchange of traffic between LMS and LNE on a gradient of 1 in 25; and the Clay Cross Tunnel which cut right through some of the more important coal seams in the locality with headings into the Tunnel bore. In the early part of the century it was not uncommon for the miners to come out into the tunnel and pass the time of day with the railway platelayers and, on occasions, practical jokes were perpetrated on visiting 'headquarters' staff.

An unusual tunnel beneath the LMS was the one which carried the River Sheaf under the entire length of Sheffield Midland Station, and still does.

Tunnels were, and continue to be, an important feature of the railway network and regular maintenance is required to ensure safety is maintained. In some locations, natural stonework forms the walls and ceiling, but in most instances brick linings, several layers thick, were put in when the tunnels were constructed, and the flow of air helps to keep the linings in good condition.

The following photographs show some of the Company's tunnels.

L. M. S.—TUNNELS OVER A MILE IN LENGTH.

Tunnel.	Section.	Length.	
		M.	Yds.
ENGLAND AND WALES—			
Totley	Mid	3	950
Standedge, Old (Single Line) (Two Tunnels) ...	L. & N. W.	3	62
„ New (Double Line)	„	3	64
Disley	Mid.	2	346
Festiniog	L. & N. W.	2	206
Cowburn	Mid.	2	182
Morley	L. & N. W.	1	1,609
Dove Holes	Mid.	1	1,224
Littleborough (Summit)	L. & Y.	1	1,125
Victoria, Waterloo (Liverpool)	L. & N. W.	1	946
Bleamoor	Mid.	1	869
Kilsby	L. & N. W.	1	666
Gildersome	„	1	571
Wapping	„	1	351
Bradway	Mid.	1	267
Sough	L. & Y.	1	255
Watford New	L. & N. W.	1	229
Halton	G. W. & L. & N. W. Jt.	1	160
Corby	Mid.	1	160
Sharnbrook	„	1	100
Glaston	„	1	82
Belsize Second	„	1	62
Watford Old	L. & N. W.	1	55
Glenfield	Mid.	1	36
Clay Cross	„	1	24
Harecastle	N. S.	1	5
SCOTLAND—			
Greenock	Cal.	1	340

Plate 9: Cast iron plates were provided a few yards before the tunnel mouth — this Totley sign is a typical example.

J. Miller

Plate 10: The south end of Sheffield Station had an unusual tunnel arrangement. The 'down' line from Chesterfield and the south burrowed beneath the Manchester lines to allow passenger trains to run into platforms 1 and 2 without having to cross the Manchester lines on the level, and thus avoid obstruction. In this view the heavily-cambered line is seen turning into the short tunnel.

G. Waite Collection

Plate 11: The low-level exit at the station end of the short tunnel, with the Midland Wyvern date panel indicating it was built in 1901. This portal is the only reminder which can be seen today when entering Sheffield from the south, the cutting having been filled in during the 1960s to 1970s.

G. Waite Collection

Plate 12: The low-level line also passed through another short tunnel before entering the station.

Author's Collection

Plate 13: An interesting view through the 49 yd. tunnels beneath Shrewsbury Road, of the entrance to Sheffield Midland Station.

D. Ibbotson

E.R.O. 21556/131

LMS

SHEFFIELD

LMS

68

Plate 14: Diggle Station, at the western end of Standedge 'twin' tunnel, opened in 1894. 'Prince of Wales' 4-6-0 No. 5805 emerges with a Manchester train. Note the signal gantry and the lowered signal arm for this train which is above the left-hand track. To the right of the picture steam can be seen puthering out of one of the single line tunnels.

D. Ibbotson

Plate 15: The eastern side of Cowburn Tunnel on the Hope Valley line in North Derbyshire. The 3F has left a trail of steam emerging from the ventilation shafts which are visible on the hillside. An interesting feature for the railway modeller is the four open carriage trucks immediately behind the tender. Note too the twin-pole telegraph poles which were a common feature in the Peak District area.

'Railways Yesteryear' Collection

Plate 16: Christleton Tunnel, near Chester, with water troughs leading to the entrance. 'Royal Scot' No. 6117 *Welsh Guardsman* hurries through.

D. Ibbotson

Plate 17: An unusual arch arrangement preceding the main Westminster Road Tunnel.

D. Ibbotson

Plate 18: 'Royal Scot' No. 6167 *The Hertfordshire Regiment* emerges from the castlated north portal of the 776yd. Shugborough Tunnel on the Western Division main line, between Colwich and Milford & Brocton, in Staffordshire. This tunnel was constructed on a curve throughout its length and was somewhat unusual in not having a single ventilation shaft. This portal was referred to by the LMS as the 'Queen' of the Company's railway tunnel fronts.
'Railways Yesteryear' Collection

Plate 19: An LMS-built Compound, No. 926, double-heads a Midland Compound south of Ambergate at the point where the Longlands Tunnel was excavated in 1930/31, to allow two additional lines to be put in (*see Plate 62 Vol. 1*).
'Railways Yesteryear' Collection

Plate 20: The 52yds. long short tunnel at Shipley with girder span added to the stone entrance, to give wider roadway capability. This is an arrangement which could be of particular interest to the model railway enthusiast with limited layout space available.

D. Ibbotson

LMS CATERING

The provision of meals for the travelling public was a perpetual requirement, whether they were served in refreshment rooms, in the dining cars or in the Company's hotels, and a wide variety of foods was required. Butchers and bakers, chefs and farm-hands were all part of the LMS Hotel & Catering Department — farm-hands at the Willesden Pig Farm, where around 145 pigs were kept, and fed on the waste food and vegetable trimmings from the dining cars, hotels and refreshment rooms. The other three trades were represented in the dining car depot kitchens, preparing endless supplies of food. More than 3 million meals were served in dining cars each year, with much of the provisions supplied to services commencing at Euston and St. Pancras.

Plate 22: This small cast plate was fixed to the nameboards at stations which had refreshment facilities — *see Volume II Plates 52 & 53.*

G. Foxley Collection

Plate 21: A 1939 view of the butcher's table and kitchen area. Note the salt-glazed brick walls and the general condition of equipment — it would probably require some attention to meet today's standards!

Author's Collection

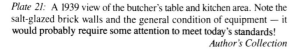

PLAYING CARDS

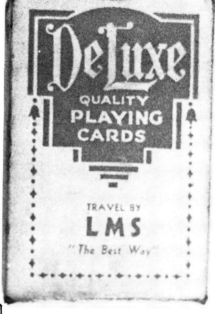

Plate 23: LMS playing cards were sold to the public for 1/- a pack from station booking offices from mid-1937. They were also advertised in the LMS Staff Magazine as a special offer for 9d if ordered on the special coupon provided, from the Executive Research Office, 203 Seymour Street, Euston. On the longer journeys passengers given to a game of cards could therefore sample and enjoy the slogans which appeared on the outer packet — 'Travel by LMS, The Best Way', and 'LMS — for Speed and Comfort', shown here.

J. Kay Collection

A
A
A
A
LMS
LMS
LMS
LMS
LMS
LMS

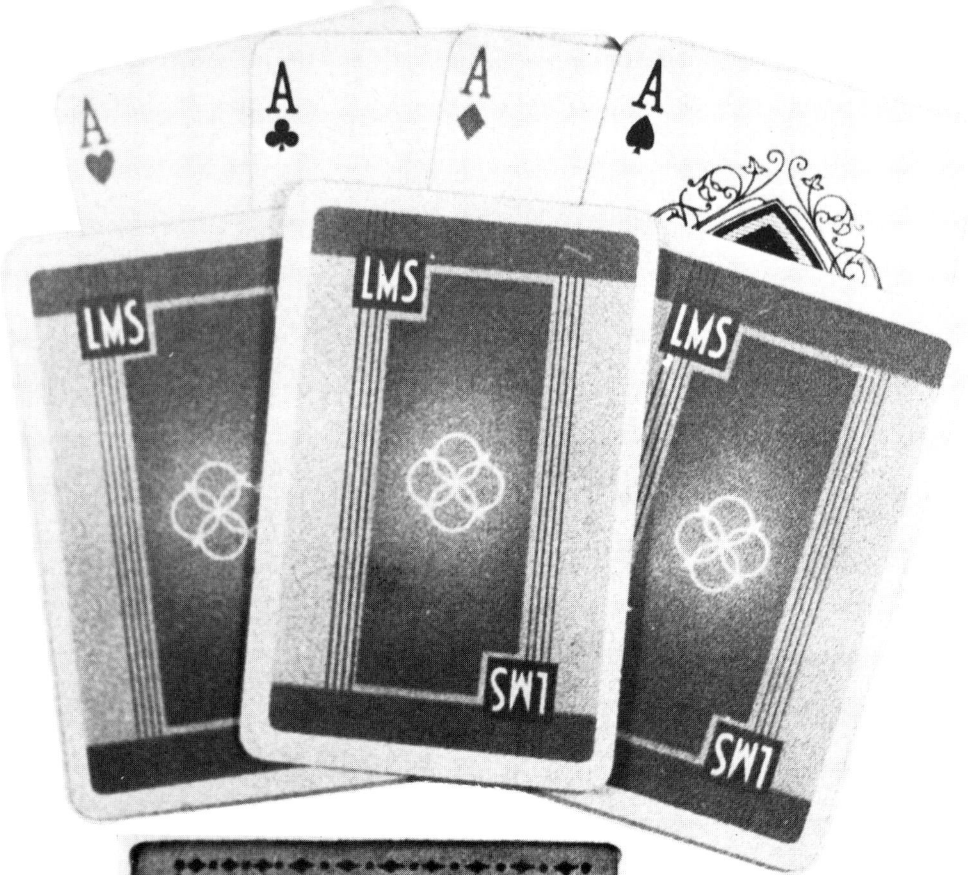

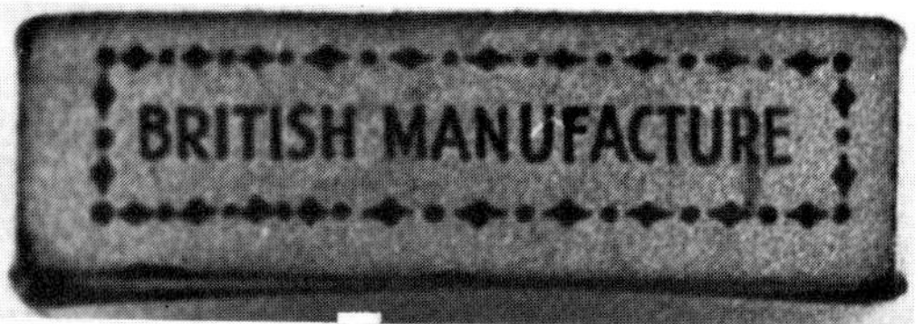

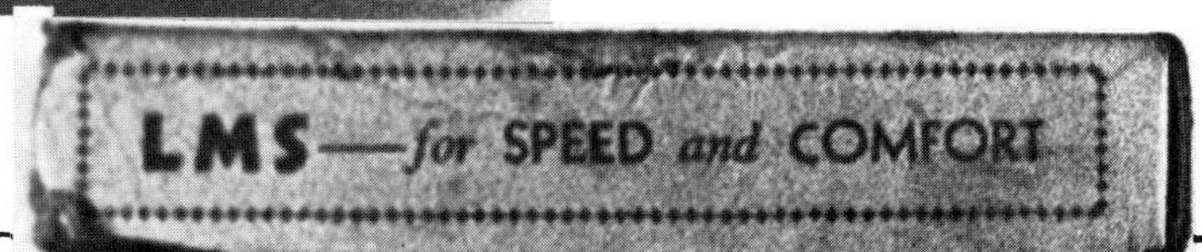

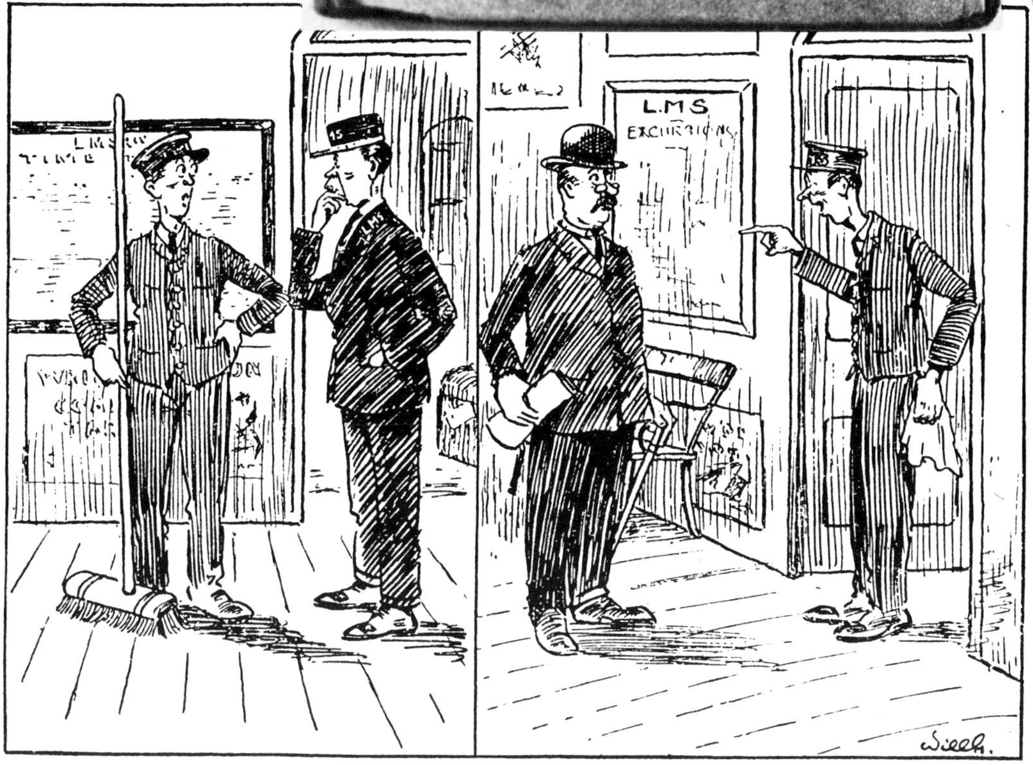

BRITISH MANUFACTURE

LMS—for SPEED and COMFORT

DeLuxe
QUALITY
PLAYING
CARDS
TRAVEL BY
LMS
"The Best Way"

L.M.S
EXCURSIONS

DISCIPLINE

Station Master, expecting District Superintendent to visit his station, enquires several times of the new porter whether he has come yet.

District Superintendent: I am the District Superintendent; where is the Station Master?

New Porter: You are, are you—you are going to catch it. The Station Master has been looking for you two hours.

LONDON MIDLAND AND SCOTTISH
RAILWAY
RULE BOOK
1933

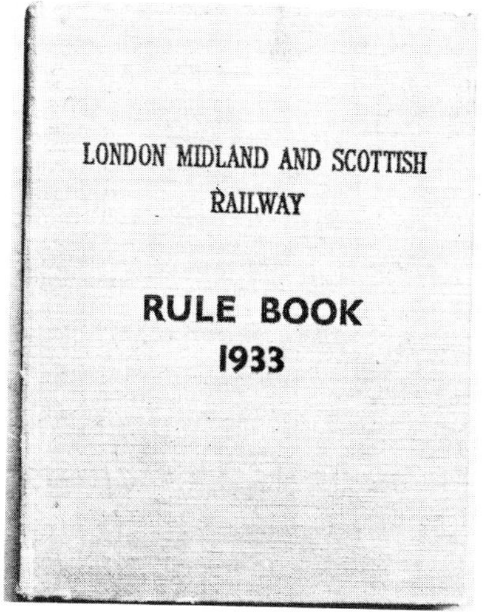

Plate 24: There's nothing like playing your cards right!

Author's Collection

LMS STAFF PUBLICATIONS

LMS Magazine

A notice was issued to LMS employees in September 1923 to announce the publication of a new illustrated monthly magazine, with the first issue in November 1923 being distributed free of charge to all employees. Thereafter, the charge for each issue was set at one penny, with annual subscriptions of one shilling, and those requiring postal despatch, the charge was two pence per issue or one shilling and sixpence per annum.

The objective was to link up the scattered units with a series of articles on different aspects of the Company, including a series on the pre-group constituent companies, and to provide also a section for items of local interest within five defined geographical areas. The editor was based in London, with sub-editors in Birmingham, Manchester, Barrow-in-Furness and Glasgow, and their duty was to collect and collate items of interest for their area sections.

Articles were paid for at a rate of 10s. 6d per 1,000 words printed, and advertisements were accepted from traders, and also from staff wishing to buy, sell or exchange items.

It became a popular medium for all employees, and it continued publication until war broke out in 1939, and the September 1939 issue became the last to be published. Thereafter, staff news was included in a new wartime publication *Carry On*.

The cover design varied over the years and the number of pages increased from the first issue of 40, to 64 for the final issue, with a handful of issues exceeding this figure.

Plate 25: Hard-binding was available for those who wished to preserve their copies. The lavish gold block title on a maroon background is seen in this plate showing a bound *Volume II*. The same block was used for the first bound volume which included the November, December, 1923 and the whole of 1924 issues, but the block was black on a maroon background.

Author's Collection

Vol. III. No. 37   The Journal of the LMS Operating Department   December, 1937

KING BORIS DRIVES
THE CORONATION SCOT

The Coronation Scot, which achieved fame in June last by reaching a maximum speed of 114 m.p.h. on a test run between Euston and Crewe, has added still further to its laurels. It has been driven by a King.

By invitation of the Company, King Boris of Bulgaria, was asked if he would like to make a special run in our latest streamlined express from Euston to Bletchley. Driving engines is more than a hobby to King Boris, it is one of the

A CHRISTMAS MESSAGE FROM THE CHIEF OPERATING MANAGER

The year which is now drawing to a close has been a momentous one in the history of the L M S Railway. Apart from the great expansion in both passenger and freight traffic

Plate 26: The heading featured No. 6200 *The Princess Royal* from *Issue No. 1* until a change to a streamlined 'Coronation' was made with the August 1937 issue.

Author's Collection

ON TIME NEWSPAPER

Within two months of the *Quota News* tabloid appearing in October 1934, the *'On Time'* newspaper in similar format appeared as the Journal of the LMS Operating Department, and continued publication until it too was superseded by the *Carry On* newspaper, issued in October 1939.

'Every train to time on every day of the week' was the theme to launch this publication, and the operating staff were encouraged to pull out all the stops to achieve this ideal. Photographs were used to give the staff up-to-date information on the measures the Company were taking to improve operating procedures. The December 1936 issue carried headlines 'World's Speed Records Smashed', an account of the Euston-Glasgow-Euston round trip which achieved a 70mph average on the return journey with Stanier Pacific No. 6201 *Princess Elizabeth*. Puntuality league tables were introduced with points awarded for early, on time and within five minutes of booked time arrivals, with standards of 1,000 points set as the 100 per cent punctual level. A section detailing the 'Month's Best Runs' was of general interest and the Somerset & Dorset line regularly featured in this section.

LMS WARTIME NEWSPAPER 'Carry On'

A replacement for the *LMS Magazine*, *Quota News* and *On Time* newspapers with the first issue shown here in *Plate 27* in October 1939. It was a free issue and remained so until the final issue in December 1947, No. 86. During the war, thirteen months were missed and if there had been no break in publication, the December 1947 issue would have been the 99th, with the 100th coinciding with the launch of the nationalised British Railways. In the event, the title *Carry On* was used for the British Railways' London Midland and Scottish Region staff newspaper/magazine. All issues up to June 1947 had been produced on white newsprint, but with the July 1947 issue a colour cover was used for the first time — red — with blues, green and purple being used for succeeding issues.

Author's Collection

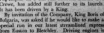

COPIES OF THIS PUBLICATION MUST NOT BE SENT ABROAD

Carry On

LMS WAR-TIME NEWSLETTER

Vol. 1   OCTOBER, 1939   No. 1

OURSELVES IN WARTIME

"CARRY ON" of which this is the first issue, is a monthly Newsletter of L M S news and activities, which it is the intention of the management shall be published each month (as near the 1st as possible) during the war emergency.

It incorporates, for the time being, the previous staff publications L M S MAGAZINE,

Our Chairman's Message to Every L M S Employee

RAILWAYS VITAL TO NATION'S CAUSE

Whatever Befall, We must Carry On
—by Lord Stamp, Chairman of the Company

RAILWAYS have never been more vital to the very life of the nation than they are in these days which find our beloved country once again at war.

In times of peace, both in prosperity and adversity, our railway system has always provided the main arteries of Britain's trade and industry. In that other great war which began twenty-five years ago, railways were transformed into a vast war machine that played an essential part in the successful conduct and the eventual triumph of our arms.

Today that grim need, which most of us surely hoped and believed would never again confront us in our lifetimes, has again arisen, and once more the railways are an active part of the national defence system.

COPIES OF THIS PUBLICATION MUST NOT BE SENT ABROAD.

CARRY ON

LMS WAR-TIME NEWSLETTER

Vol 4.   NOVEMBER, 1943   No. 37

The President, Sir William Wood, writes

An open letter to You

I AM sorry it is not possible for me to write a letter addressed to each of the 240,000 men and women working on the LMS Railway and to the 38,000 now with the Armed Forces or temporarily working elsewhere at the

The letters I see from those of us who unfortunately are prisoners war or are in outlying places abroad with the discomforts of tropic climates and boring conditions, spea almost without exception of their eagerness to keep themselves in touc

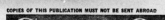

Plate 28: The block heading was changed with issue No. 9 and it was not until the introduction of the colour cover that the heading block was again changed, as shown in *Plate 265*.

Author's Collection

Sub-Editor.—W. W. SHARP, General Manager's Office, 2, Euston Grove

Bletchley

The Nightworkers' League team have played four games to date and some curious scores have resulted as ... st.

THE annual meeting for the distribution of awards to ...

Sub-Editor.—W. R. DUTHIE, Office of Deputy General Manager for Scotland, Glasgow

Aberdeen

THAT keen interest is still being maintain... ambulance work was shown by the increas... new members enrolling at the open... ...ss on Sunday, Septemb...

The following donations were allocated to the vario...

Sub-Editor—G. A. GRIBBLE, D.G.M.O., Curzon Street, Birmingham

Sub-Editor—A. K. LAWSON, District Goods Manager's Office, Rates Dept., Room 90, Hunt's Bank, Manchester

Sub-Editor—E. D. SHEPHERD, D.G.M.O., Wellington Street, Leeds

Sub-Editor—DUNCAN GALBRAITH, Office of Deputy General Manager for Scotland, Glasgow

LMS Football Challenge Cup Competition
(Scottish Section)

The following table sh... ...ition of the various club... ...

Plate 29: Within a few months, the local interest sections were given distinctive headings and these are seen on the left. The London section heading remained the same when, in October 1925, the designs were changed to those on the right side. The four page headings were typical of the special interest sections which had a Company-wide interest. The section headings were changed as time progressed until, during the latter years of publication, simple block lettering was used.

Author's Collection

MIDLAND DIVISION AMBULANCE CENTRE

...list of ambulance classes which ...Midland Division sin... ...should ...

Br
C
Foo
Am
soc
Lor
Offi

SOME GAMES AND PUZZLES FOR THE XMAS PARTY

By "Jester"

IN this article the reader will find instruction in the playing of a number of games suitable for indoor amusement. After studying the information given no one should experience any difficulty in keeping up an ...ing's fun. Moreover, it would be an excellent thing ... persons in a family made themselves pro... ...games mentioned, as they would ...cial amusements.

shown in Fig. 2 and invite the strong person to stand in front of you and, grasping one of your wrists in each hand, to pull them apart. If he has not tried this before the result will surprise him—his utmost endeavours will be in vain. The next trick requires an empty matchbox. Stand the tray on its side and place the case crosswise on this (Fig. 3). Challenge anyone to smash the box by striking downwards on to it with a hand held edgeways. Nine times out of ten the tray will give way and the two parts fly apart none the worse for the blow. A very amusing trick is performed a...

THE 1925 Sheet Almanack is now on sale. Printed on art paper, it contains a useful table of L.M.S. statistics; President's New Year's Message; Membership of District Councils; Calendar 1925, and illustrations of a modern LMS Express, Gourock, Monsal Dale, and Keswick. All subscribers of not less than 3d. per annum will be presented with a free copy annually. Copies may be had from the General Secretary at the following rates:—1 copy, 1½d.; 12 copies, 1s. 4d.; 25, 2s. 3d.; 50, 4s.; 100, 7s. 3d. Mounted, varnished, eye-letted and corded, 1 copy, 4d.; 6 copies,

November 8. Mr. Wm. Lamb presided. The Secretary (Mr. G. Hewitt) gave an interesting report of the Birmingham Conference. The special Membership Campaign proposals were considered and co-operation promised, and arrangements made for meetings in the district. The next meeting to be held at Carstairs. On November 7 Mr. B. Oldham gave a lantern lecture in St. Michael's Parish Room. Chairman, Rev. Ernest Elliott, A.T.S. The local arrangements were made by Mr. J. W. Elding.

Leeds District.—Well-attended meeting held at Leeds,

QUOTA LEAGUES

In January 1934, Mr Ashton Davies, the Chief Commercial Manager, introduced a 'new game' in which all the employees could participate, called 'Getting the Quota'. He drew a parallel with the game of golf when he introduced the new game, 'I have set a standard of passenger and merchandise receipts which we hope to attain this year, and which is the line quota, and in the same way as bogey is based on the figure for each hole, so is the line quota figure split up amongst stations and individuals so that the sum total of their efforts may secure the final result.'

To make the game interesting, a calendar quota score card was supplied to each passenger and goods station upon which the daily achievements could be recorded against the quota, and every individual was encouraged to exert maximum effort towards achieving their 'quota'. Results were monitored and league tables within the operating districts added a further competitive edge. In October 1934, the LMS introduced a tabloid newspaper *Quota News*, and this carried the reports of progress and articles of interest relating to new services, letters of appreciation, etc. *Quota News* was discontinued at the outbreak of war in 1939, and from October, 1939 *Quota* items were carried in the LMS Wartime Newspaper *Carry On*.

VOL. III. NO. 16   THE JOURNAL OF THE **LMS** COMMERCIAL DEPARTMENT   JANUARY, 1936

THE "COMMERCIAL" NEW YEAR
The "Matterhorn" of our Ambition

By Ashton Davies
Chief Commercial Manager

IF ever the time comes when the Commercial Department sits back and says it is satisfied—then there will be something radically wrong with the Commercial Department. For this reason I am not going to say that I am satisfied with the result of the trading for the year that has just finished, but I do want to say, and to say most sincerely, that I *am* satisfied with the wholehearted efforts that have been put forth by the staff to improve the commercial prosperity of this great undertaking.

The full results of the year's trading

payment of a nominal registration fee of half-a-crown per consignment.

It is hardly necessary for me to point out the commercial possibilities of these developments. Back to 1929 is a phrase that has been stressed so often that there may be a danger that it is becoming *just a phrase* and nothing more. I am relying on you to make it more than a phrase, to make it in fact a reality.

We have the service and I am convinced that in the staff of the Commercial Department, from the lowest to the highest, we have the men to put that service over. As you all know the Quota system has been devised as a means of assessing our progress and as a spur to endeavour. Like all such systems it has its weaknesses.

Plate 30: Quota News page style. Author's Collection

Plate 31: The Northern Division 'Quota' Competition Presentations held on 9th March 1937 at the Central Hotel, Glasgow. The three gentlemen behind the cups are (left to right) Mr Charles Ker (Chairman of the Scottish Local Quota Committee), Mr J. Ballantyne, (Chief Officer for Scotland), and Sir Harold Hartley (Vice-President of the LMS). The remaining 19 individuals and others present were there to collect the three cups for topping the Northern Division 'Quota' Leagues, and the 45 shields for those topping the individual District Leagues.

National Railway Museum

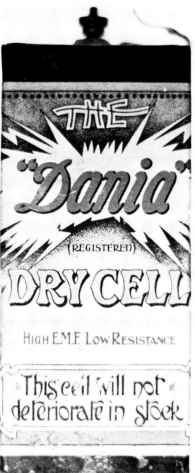

THE "Dania" (REGISTERED) DRY CELL

HIGH E.M.F. LOW RESISTANCE

This cell will not deteriorate in stock

L.M.S.R.

Date

C.S.

Plate 32: A dry-cell battery bought in quantity by the LMS, and having a variety of uses.

J. Kay Collection

LMS

Pull together!

SUPPORT THE INDUSTRY
THAT SUPPORTS YOU

IT LIES GREATLY IN
YOUR POWER TO DO SO

Get Customers —
Please Customers

Plate 33: A cast-iron stair tread commonly found on signal cabin stairways.

G. Foxley Collection

Plate 34: Even enamelled wash bowls provided in hotels were embellished with the Company initials.

G. Foxley Collection

1—2/32.   E.R.O. 21947.

L. M. S. R.

Via Carlisle & L. M. S.,
(Caledonian Section)

LONDON MIDLAND & SCOTTISH RAILWAY
(Midland Division)
HORTICULTURAL SOCIETY

MEMBERSHIP CARD

This card is issued in return for the Annual Subscription of One Shilling to June 30th, 1943, and is the only receipt given

NOT TRANSFERABLE.

Member's Signature ....

.... Dept............................Station

S. R. CRUNKHORN,
Hon. Gen. Sec., Derby.

Nº 1246   P.T.O.

L. M. & S. R.
Wrenbury

FOR MEMBERS ONLY.

THE DERBY SWEEPSTAKE

RUN WEDNESDAY, JUNE 5th, 1946.
ROWSLEY L.M.S. AREA STAFF OUTING.

— PRIZES VALUE —

1st—£20.   2nd—£10.   3rd—£5.
4th—£2.   Last Horse—£1/10/-
Other Runners—£1.

Promoters—Committee of the above.

Winners notified.

Tickets 6d. each.

Book of 22—10/-   Nº 90

H. Roberts & Son, Printers, Matlock.

LMS STONE QUARRYING

The LMS inherited the stone quarries at Caldon Low from the North Staffordshire Railway, and continued to work them until late 1934. Early records indicate that limestone was quarried at Caldon Low, a bleak moorland area in North Staffordshire between Ashbourne and Leek, prior to 1776. Quarry owners in the area were obliged under an Agreement between themselves and the Trent & Mersey Canal Navigation Company, to supply certain quantities of limestone to the Canal Company on a royalty basis, but in 1841 it was decided this arrangement could no longer continue. A new Agreement was made enabling the Canal Company to quarry the stone themselves, subject to royalty payments to the various quarry owners.

In 1846, the Trent & Mersey Canal Company was merged into the North Staffordshire Railway Company and they continued to quarry the stone until the London, Midland & Scottish Railway Company took over operations from 1st January 1923. Around this time, the annual tonnage was approximately 200,000 tons, but some six years later little more than 165,000 tons left the quarry.

Messrs Hadfields (Hope & Caldon Low Quarries) Ltd., a subsidiary company of Derbyshire Stone Ltd., and they continued to work the deposits throughout the remainder of the LMS period to 1947 and beyond. The limestone was exceedingly hard with a crushing strain of 31,000lbs. per square inch, and suitable for furnace stone and chemical purposes, railway ballast, concrete aggregate, limestone powder for chemical purposes, and tar macadam. The works at the quarries were capable of producing approximately 1,500 tons per day.

12th July 1938, was a special day at Caldon Low Quarry, and at Euston Station, London, also.

Lord Stamp, Chairman of the LMS, made a speech from the Board Room at Euston Station which was transmitted by land-wire and loudspeaker to an invited audience assembled at the Caldon Low Quarry. The official party, which included Sir Francis Joseph, a Director of the LMS, then witnessed a ten-ton blast of black explosive, set off by Lord Stamp at Euston using a firing switch to operate an electrical relay at the quarry, which closed the circuit between the mains supply of electricity and the cables carrying the current to the explosive charges. It was estimated that more than 100,000 tons of limestone was blasted and from this it was intended that a suitable piece would be used to form a foundation stone for the proposed new Euston Station; alas this was never built by the LMS.

After the blast the official parties were transported to the LMS North Stafford Hotel, Stoke-on-Trent, where they were entertained by the Directors of Hadfield's.

There were other sides to the quarry operations. In 1906 the North Stafford had opened up a cave which was full of stalactites, stalagmites and fossils, and they fitted this out with stairways and electric lighting, and it proved to be a great tourist attraction. The Company also produced some fine coloured postcards of this cave and on their nearby Leek & Manifold Railway Station at Waterhouses, they added the 'command' — 'Alight for Froghall Quarries' — Froghall Quarries were in fact those at Caldon Low.

There were three locomotives used in the quarries until the mid-1930s, two dating from 1877 built by Hughes & Co of Loughborough, and a third from W. J. Bagnall Ltd., of Stafford in 1901. All were scrapped in May 1936.

In the period to 1930, the Quarry contributed to LMS profits in all but one year, 1926, when a loss of £626 was recorded for the year. Tonnage was 108,013 tons, the lowest in this period, most probably affected by the General Strike that year when quarry workers would probably have identified with the coal mining dispute. In the last year of LMS operation, 1934, a mere 37,571 tons were quarried, but from gross receipts of £8,615, a profit of £2,623 was recorded.

Between 1929, when tonnage was 165,201 and 1933, with 27,409 tons, a large number of employees left the quarries.

Plate 35: The outer cover of a brochure produced specially for Lord Stamp's long range ignition of the blast at Caldon Low Quarry.

Dr J. Hollick Collection

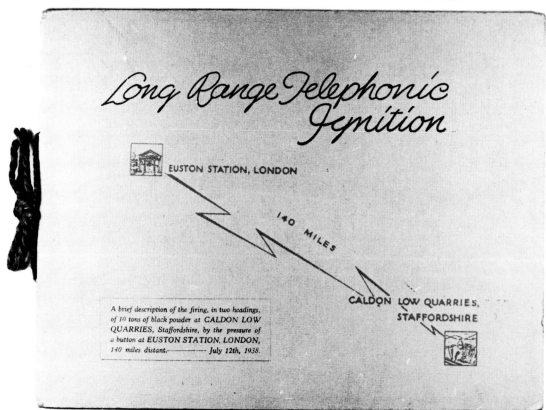

Plate 36: A plan of the twin-tunnel detonation arrangement in the brochure.
Dr J. Hollick Collection

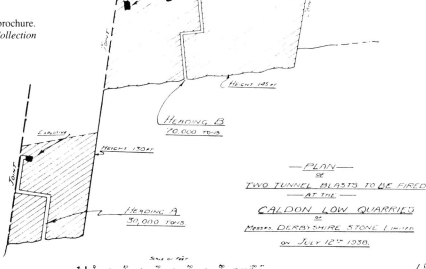

Plate 37: An aerial view of the Caldon Low Quarry, with the LMS lines in the foreground to facilitate movement of stone to all parts of the country.
Dr J. Hollick Collection

Plate 38: One of the Caldon Low Quarry engines — *Toad* — loaded on board Mr Wedgwood's steam lorry for transportation to the LMS works at Stoke-on-Trent for repairs. Stoke Works closed in 1927.
J. Hollick

Plate 39: An attempt at preserving this former Midland Railway 0-4-4T, No. 6, seen here inside the Derby Locomotive Works paint shop in May 1931, foundered soon afterwards and it was broken up.

G. Coltas

SMOKING
STRICTLY PROHIBITED
ON THESE PREMISES

NOTICE
ANY PERSON FOUND TAKING FIREWOOD
OR ANY OTHER PROPERTY BELONGING TO THE
COMPANY FROM THESE PREMISES WILL
BE DISMISSED FROM THE SERVICE AND
BE LIABLE TO PROSECUTION
BY ORDER

Plate 42 (opposite): Compound 4-4-0 No. 1111 inside Liverpool (Edge Hill) Shed in 1932.

G. Coltas

Plate 43 (opposite): One of ten Hughes 4-6-4T engines built in 1924 by the LMS at Horwich to a Lancashire & Yorkshire Railway design. No. 11111 is seen at Horwich Works in June 1938.

N. R. E. Williams

LMS
1

Plate 40: Former Midland 2-4-0 No. 1 at Castle Bromwich on 3rd June 1925.

W. L. Good

LOCOMOTIVES — NOS. 1 TO 11111

By way of variation the engines carrying all 'ones'.

Plate 41: No. 11, a 1930 Derby-built 2-6-2T, seen here at Bescot Shed at the end of the LMS period.

W. T. Stubbs

A former Midland Railway 2-4-0 carried the number 11 whilst there were also 2-6-2T engines carrying numbers 1 and 111, during the LMS period.

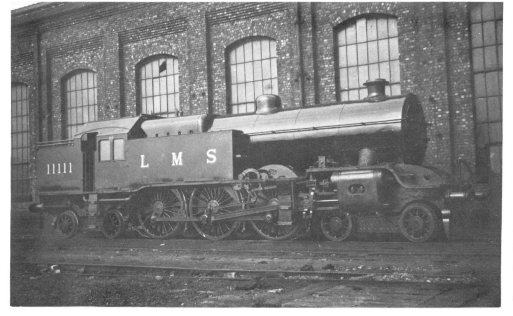

M. F. No. 4

LONDON MIDLAND AND SCOTTISH RAILWAY COMPANY.

NOTICE TO ENGINEMEN

Engines emitting Smoke, Blowing off Steam and Whistling.

Numerous complaints are being received about engines emitting dense volumes of smoke, blowing off steam, and also whistling unnecessarily.

Enginemen are hereby requested to exercise care and so prevent such complaints.

CHIEF GENERAL SUPERINTENDENT.

Derby, December, 1926.

McCorquodale & Co. Ltd., Printers, London and Newton.

SNOW HAZARD

One of the natural hazards which could play havoc with railway services, and without a great deal of warning! Each winter one or more lines were seriously affected, and on rare occasions a line would be closed, and a train stranded. Lines in Scotland were the most frequent casualties, with those through high ground in the rest of the mainland cut off at times. Snowploughs for attachment to locomotives were maintained at most of the locomotive depots which were in or had engine-turns in the most likely areas to be affected. The largest ploughs were the four built by the Midland Railway on old double-bogie tender frames and allocated in pairs to Hellifield and Carlisle depots. These were 33ft. long and each weighed approximately 26 tons, and they were specifically for use on the bleak Settle & Carlisle stretch of line. Normally two freight engines were marshalled between the two outward facing ploughs — the engines were those fitted with permanent back cabs on the tender. In addition to the enginemen, an acting inspector from the Motive Power Section, a Permanent Way Inspector, a Traffic Inspector, a telegraph clerk and a cook travelled in the riding van accommodation within the ploughs.

At certain points where the hillside rose above the line, there was always the danger of loose snow blowing on to the railway and, to overcome this, snow screens were built from old sleepers and were effective in minimising blown snow.

Stories of blizzards disrupting the railways were always told with relish by those who had had the experience, so much so that in the remoter hamlets and villages they are part of the folklore.

The four ex-Midland ploughs were unique on the LMS, but there were many more which were bolted to a locomotive front to serve the same purpose, and some of these are illustrated here. In late 1934, the Company commissioned twenty four new engine snowploughs for use on the more mountainous and exposed sections of line to replace some of the older and obsolete equipment. Fifteen of these — known as the 'all steel nose' type — were allocated for work principally on the Highland Section between Perth and Inverness, and further north to Wick. The remaining nine ploughs were allocated between the South Wales area, the Buxton district, and the Carlisle to Hellifield stretch, to replace the former Midland ploughs.

The year 1947 will be remembered by many for the very heavy snowfalls which caused much disruption to the transportation systems, and the LMS carried out experiments on the Ashbourne to Buxton line using a wagon-mounted jet engine exhaust to blow the snow away (*see Volume I, Plate 63*).

Plate 44: A snowed-in train, the victim of drifting snow, in the Peak District.
Author's Collection

Plate 45: A line of ploughs stored at Perth motive power depot in 1930. These were of wooden frame construction with steel wedge pieces — types replaced by the all-steel nose type in 1934.

G. Coltas

Plate 46: A 2-6-4T, No. 2344 heads a Tring to Euston train from Berkhamsted in snowy conditions on 6th March 1947.

H. C. Casserley

THE AIM OF THE
CHIEF OPERATING MANAGER'S
DEPARTMENT

EVERY TRAIN
TO TIME
ON
EVERY DAY
OF THE WEEK

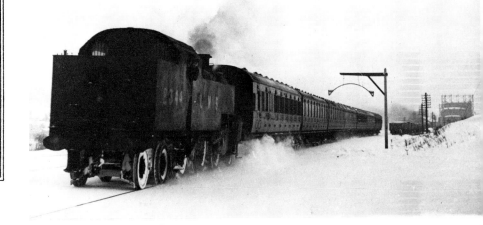

Plate 47: An express for Euston headed by 'Jubilee' No. 5666 *Cornwallis* on the 'up' fast line at Berkhamsted, shortly after Nos. 2344, seen in the previous photograph, had passed.

H. C. Casserley

E.R.O. 21556/57

L M S

EUSTON

BEWARE OF TRAINS.

Plate 48: One of the smaller ploughs fitted to a Midland 4F carrying the early Buxton shed plate — 20.

Author's Collection

SLEET VANS

Plate 50 (opposite upper): The interior showing the de-icing fluid 50 gallon tank and pipework through the floor. The internal bulkheads have been removed.

Author's Collection

Plate 51 (opposite lower): The de-icing shoe-beam is a wooden trough with brushes in contact with the outside electrified rail. The circular pad for the centre rail is raised off the rail. There is a great deal of pipework coming from the end of this vehicle, most probably to allow it to work as part of one of the electric train formations. The buffers here are longer than those fitted at the other end — *see Plate 49.*

Author's Collection

Plate 49:   Numbered in the Departmental Stock, this vehicle was kept at Stonebridge Park for de-icing work on the electrified lines out of Euston. A number of similar ex-L&NWR non-corridor carriages were numbered in the departmental series — this 45ft. vehicle was built to Diagram 226, one compartment with 5 first class seats, three × 8 third-class compartments, and a lavatory to each compartment.

Author's Collection

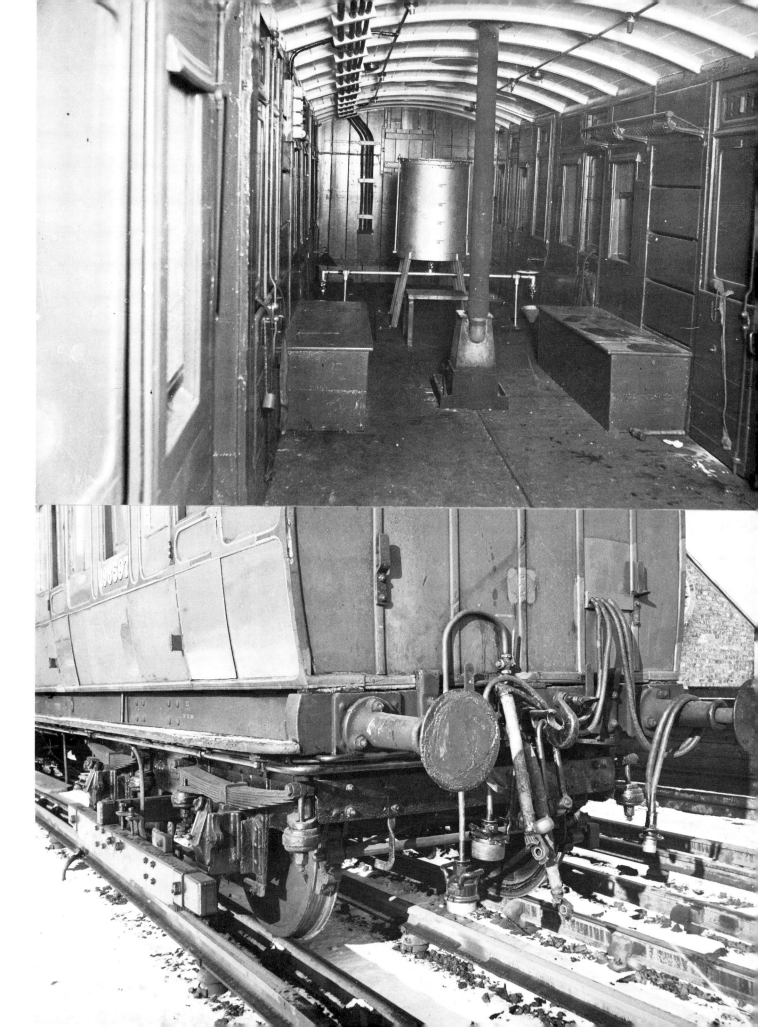

AUTOMATIC "STONE" SIGNALS

LMS trains leaving Loch Awe for Oban entered a stretch of single line which was one of the most potentially hazardous on the whole system. The line through the Pass of Brander had the sides of Ben Cruachan rise steeply on one side, and a deep stretch of water on the other, and there was always the danger of boulders rolling down the hillside and on to the railway, particularly in cold or wet weather, or when the sheep were scrambling about.

Automatic stone signals in the pass gave warning of any landslides or snow avalanches which endangered the railway line, and they were spaced at intervals, each with an 'up' and a 'down' arm for two-way operations, except for the first signals at each end of the section, which had only one arm each. The stone signals were connected by a number of wires forming a screen which ran alongside the railway on the hill side of the line. The screen was not unlike an ordinary wire boundary fence, except it was double the height, and the wire strands were wider apart. So long as the screen wires were not broken by stones coming down the mountainside, the signals remained in the clear position, but when one or more was damaged, this was sufficient to set the signals to danger.

Every alternate wire in the screen passed the first signal post and was connected with the second post, and in the event that a signal was at danger, the train proceeded slowly with the fireman walking ahead of the train to ascertain if there were any obstructions on the line. The stone signals were also connected to warning bells in the signal box and watchman's house at Awe Crossing, to the ganger's house at Falls of Cruachan, and in the ganger's house at Bridge of Awe, and when the bells sounded, the line had to be examined without delay.

The automatic stone signals were put in by the Caledonian Railway and remain in use today.

Plate 52: One of the bi-directional stone signals located on the water side of the line.

P. Tatlow

Plate 53: The signal wire arrangement, one of several such installations in the Pass of Brander, located on the mountain side of the line.

P. Tatlow

TOTON MARSHALLING YARDS

The village of Toton lies a few miles south-west of Nottingham, and almost equidistant east of Derby, to the south and south-west, Leicester and Birmingham respectively; to the north, Chesterfield and Sheffield. Much of the coal and minerals for these centres passed through the vast acreage of sidings which grew as the Midland Railway prospered. Prior to 1901, the sidings were flat and wagons were shunted by either locomotives or horses, and some seventy of these were required to keep the wagons rolling. In 1901 what was believed to be the first 'hump' or 'gravitational' arrangement in Great Britain, was made by the Midland Railway at Toton. By 1934, the sidings were said to be 138 in number with an aggregate mileage of 55 miles.

There were two yards, the 'down' and the 'up'. The 'down' yard handled mostly empty traffic, whilst the 'up' dealt with loaded vehicles. Because of its central location on the Midland Division of the LMS, it was an ideal focal point for the various centres of industry, particularly the colleries, to despatch complete trains to Toton where they would be broken and shunted, before despatch to the various destinations. Coal, for example, was mined all around the Midlands and North Midlands area, and there were different qualities and characteristics of the individual colliery areas, but seldom did a train of wagons arrive at Toton and continue on to its destinations, without either some vehicles being taken off for other destinations, or further wagons being added. Similarly, trains of empty wagons were brought to Toton for sorting and subsequent despatch to the owning colleries or other industries, although after pooling of wagons was brought in, less destination sorting of empties took place, other than for specific types of vehicle.

With siding reorganisation and simplification, and use of the 'hump', handling capacity increased considerably. There were 275 trains arriving and departing with as many as 10,000 wagons in a twenty four hour period, with similar numbers departing, ensuring that Toton fulfilled its role as a major marshalling centre on the LMS. Work shifts continued around the clock, employing 230 in the shunting grades, and there were twelve shunting engines in the yards at peak times. Some 560 enginemen, fitters and maintenance men were employed in the Motive Power Department, preparing and handling engines for the departing trains, seldom less than 140 a day.

The 'hump' installed in 1901 continued in use until 1939 and as the wagons came over the 'hump' at a slow pace, they were uncoupled by shunters on the yard side of the hump. Pointsmen guided each 'cut' of wagons (a maximum of six) through a series of points and into the siding corresponding to the number which had been chalked on the first wagon in each 'cut' by a shunter prior to 'humping'. This man had to read each wagon destination label and chalk accordingly.

Further modernisation and mechanisation was carried out by the LMS in the early months of 1939 when new control and humping rooms were built, the first sections beyond the 'humps' more steeply graded, and Fröhlich mechanical rail brakes were installed. The gradient from the 'hump' was set at 1 in 18 downhill to the first point, known as the 'King' point. From here, both lines continued down a further section at 1 in 72 to the next points; 'Queen' points. The next section to the 'Jack' points also included the mechanical rail brakes set between the rails. The fan of sidings beyond were laid in saucer fashion with gradients of 1 in 302 down and uphill, either side of a level section.

Chalking of the leading wagon in each 'cut' was still necessary prior to humping, but thereafter the 'hump room' operator could set the necessary points to clear a road into the appropriate siding for each 'cut', thus eliminating the various pointsmen in the yard. In addition, the 'hump room' operator indicated by pressing appropriate buttons on the control panel, the siding number and the number of wagons in each 'cut', and this information was printed out on a moving paper roll in the control room. From this information, and by assessing the speed of the wagons moving down the 'hump' and the

Plate 54: A night-time scene in May 1939 during the modernisation programme work. A line of wagons waiting to be pushed over the first 'gravitational hump'. Newly installed colour-light signal is seen on the left. A number '3' chalk mark is just visible on the lower end plank (right side).

British Railways

Plate 55: A view from the new control room showing a 'cut' of wagons moving down the gradient. The new 'hump room' is well illuminated. The dark building on the right, and the cabin between this and the 'hump room', are signal cabin structures which served as pointsmen's boxes until they were rendered redundant under the modernisation programme. Both are in the course of being dismantled. The yard lighting can be seen as very effective giving a wide spread of illumination. Only a short while after this picture was taken in May 1939, the wartime conditions caused much of this lighting to be reduced considerably to prevent easy identification from marauding enemy aircraft.

British Railways

distance into the siding they had to travel, a rail-brake operator in the elevated control room could apply rail-brake pressure sufficient to steady the wagons into the siding.

The section between the 'King' point and the rail-brakes was track-circuited to an illuminated panel in the control room, to ensure control of moving wagons was maintained during adverse weather and later wartime blackout conditions.

Big improvements in operation also came from the introduction of 0-6-0 diesel shunting engines in the mid-1930s, not least in that they could carry sufficient diesel fuel for several days of operation — unlike the steam shunters which had to return to the shed at least once each day on what was dead mileage and a time-consuming operation.

New colour-light signalling was also installed as part of the modernisation as well as improved yard lighting. Loud speaker communication between the 'hump room', control tower and various positions in the yard was also provided for use when movements other than 'humping' were necessary, or additional audible communication became necessary. Toton locomotive sheds were the home of many of the 33 Garratt-type engines built by Beyer Peacock for the LMS between 1927 and 1930, to handle the heavy coal and mineral traffic emanating from the Toton Yards, and these were a common sight on the line

south to London, to Birmingham, and to the north of Toton up the Erewash Valley line.

The locomotive depot consisted of three large sheds with a repair shop, stores and offices, a wheel drop, electrically-operated coaling plant and mechanical ash-lifting plant, and a Paterson water softening system capable of providing 2½ million gallons of soft water for locomotives per week.

Another facility provided at Toton was the wagon repair shops with crippled wagon sidings for receipt of any vehicle requiring attention. The workshops were equipped with modern machines to allow repairs to be undertaken whatever the nature.

In addition to motive power personnel and shunting grades, there were around 400 other employees in the wagon repair section, a signal and telegraph section, and the clerical grades, bringing the total for the Toton Yards to approximately 1,200.

The staff were drawn from the local towns and villages, Sandiacre, Stapleford, Long Eaton, Chilwell and Sawley, and in each of these areas the Company had one or two employees whose job it was to cycle around the locality during the night knocking-up those employees who had asked for a call when on early duty, particularly footplate staff whose clocking-on times were at odd times. The 'knocker-up', as he was known, had a lonely task!

Plate 56 (opposite upper): A view looking towards the 'hump room', with an 0-6-0 diesel shunter pushing wagons over the 'hump'. The circular 'hump-shunt' signal above the 'hump room' roof has a row of three lights shining vertically, indicating 'Hump at normal speed'. Provision was also made for three lights to shine diagonally, to indicate 'Hump at slow speed', and when three lights shone horizontally that was the signal to 'Stop shunting'. The sharp gradient over the 'hump' can be seen to good effect in this view. The Erewash Valley main lines ran through the centre of the Toton complex, and regular express passenger services between St. Pancras and the north, which were not scheduled to call at Derby or Nottingham, used the line, which is situated between the line of wagons to the right and the 'hump'.

British Railways

Plate 57 (opposite lower): This view shows one of the Fröhlich mechanical rail-brakes, a patented German piece of equipment, which applied pressure to the inside edge of the wheel tyres to retard the speed of a wagon sufficiently to ensure it ran the appropriate distance into the reception siding. Four of these were provided in each of the 'up' and 'down' yards, this view being in the 'down' yard. The 'down' yard control room is seen to the right.

British Railways

Plate 58: A general view of the 'down' yard from the control room, with the newly-ballasted areas showing the extent of the track alterations during the modernisation programme. In this view, photographed on 31st July 1939, the Toton motive power depot is seen at the far end of the yard.

British Railways

Plate 59: The interior of the control room, with the operator on the left controlling the rail-brakes and the points operator at the far end of the room. The Controller watches proceedings from the comfort of a chair.

British Railways

Plate 60: A view of the yard at Toton motive power depot on 16th July 1930, before modernisation, with a variety of freight engine classes represented. Toton carried an allocation of almost 200 engines, including the small 0-6-0T and diesel shunters.

V. R. Anderson Collection

Plate 61: Beyer Garratt No. 4981 heads a long train of private owner coal wagon empties through Elstree, en route to Toton from the London area, a regular turn to balance the outward workings from Toton to London with full wagons.

G. Coltas

COAL TRAFFIC HANDLING

In 1929 the LMS carried more than 84 million tons of coal, 33 per cent of all coal output in the mainland. A total of 5.8 million tons was used by the Company's own locomotives, the remaining seventy-odd million bringing revenue to the Company.

There were many ways of handling the mineral, not least the provision of tall coaling towers at the main locomotive depots in the early 1930s. Substantial quantities however, were often handled by hand, and although the following photographs were taken in the late Midland Railway period, they serve to show two methods of bulk handling employed in the London area where some 3.3 million tons was handled through LMS wharves.

Plate 62: Wagons were moved by traverser and placed over open drops and the load discharged, either through doors in the floor, or side doors, and this would entail manual handling to completely empty the vehicle — and this was done religiously so that none was wasted. The arrangement is clearly shown here — part of the roof has been removed.

V. R. Anderson Collection

(826—Home Empty Label.)

Wagon No._____   Owner_____

Date Received_____   Date Returned _____

From _____

THIS WAGON MUST BE SENT
HOME EMPTY

Via_____

Due off L. M. & S. Line before 4.0 p.m. on _____ 192

Plates 63 & 64: Two views of the wagon tilt arrangement for transferring a load of coal into waiting barges for movement by water. The upper view is at Cambridge Street barging depot on the Regents Canal, and the other is at Poplar Wharf on the River Thames — very much bygone scenes, but in use throughout the LMS period in much the same manner as shown here.

V. R. Anderson Collection

Plate 65: This view of the Cambridge Street coal depot near to St. Pancras Station shows the roadway arrangement for collecting the coal, with carts backed beneath the railway wagon level. The larger carts are Midland-owned, but there are several vehicles which were known as the London coal cart type. Second from the left is one such vehicle, and although the sides and curved end look less substantial than the railway vehicles, they were sturdy enough to survive coal carrying. The front was sloped forward, to allow the bags of coal to be stood and kept in an upright position during deliveries. The private coal traders often used two vehicles together, and in hilly areas, one horse would be unhitched, and it would assist the other vehicle up the incline, thereafter, both horses returning to take the second cart forward in the same way.

V. R. Anderson Collection

REGISTERED BY THE
1942
■ STANDARD I4 TONS ■
164064
L M S

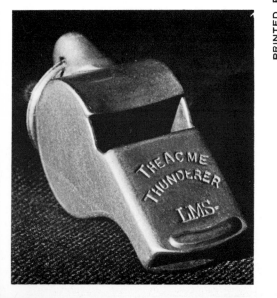

1—2/32

E.R O. 28705

L. M. & S. R. _____ Station, _____ 19

The following wagons have been stopped here for repairs.

NOTICE—When Wagons, for the purpose of repair, are required to be shunted into and out of Railway Companies' Sidings $\frac{\text{and}}{\text{or}}$ into and out of premises in the occupation of Private Wagon Repairers, a minimum charge of 1/- per Wagon will be made for such services.

Siding Rent will be chargeable to the Owner, or his Agent, in respect of standing room for any wagon detained at a Station or Siding for repairs, at the rate of 6d per wagon per day, which will be calculated from the expiration of three days (exclusive of the date of the Advice Note, Sundays, and Bank Holidays), from the time the wagon is stopped, and terminate when the wagon is repaired to the Company's satisfaction and labelled for despatch.

Before proceeding with the repair of the truck specified below, the Workman must produce this advice to, and put himself in direct communication with, the Station Agent or Principal Officer in charge, and satisfy himself that the necessary arrangements have been made for his proceeding with the repairs in safety. He must also observe the instructions for the protection of Employees of Private Wagon Repairing Firms.

PRINTED PAPER RATE.

OWNER.	Number of Wagon.	PRINCIPAL DEFECTS.	Empty or Loaded.	DESTINATION.

*—*Please arrange for the above mentioned and any other defects to be repaired.*
* —*L. M. & S. Railway Company will carry out repairs.*
*—*Strike out clause not appplicable.*

_____ *Agent.*

Plate 66: An appropriate name, 'The Acme Thunderer', as those who were near to the guard when he blew the whistle would vouch for. It had to be a penetrating shrill sound, to be heard long and hard above the normal station noise.

G. Foxley Collection

Plate 67: Novelty's cylinder.
Author's Collection

Plate 68: The commemorative tablet which explained the unusual piece of machinery seen in *Plate 67.*
Author's Collection

ONE OF THE TWO CYLINDERS OF THE LOCOMOTIVE "NOVELTY" BUILT BY BRAITHWAITE AND ERICSSON IN 1829 FOR THE FAMOUS RAINHILL TRIALS OF THE SAME YEAR. THE COMPANION. CYLINDER IS IN THE SOUTH KENSINGTON MUSEUM HAVING BEEN INCORPORATED IN A MODEL OF THE ENGINE MADE THERE. PRESENTED BY THE PRESCOT AND DISTRICT GAS COMPANY TO THE LONDON, MIDLAND AND SCOTTISH RAILWAY COMPANY FOR PERMANENT EXHIBITION AT RAINHILL STATION IN THE CENTENARY YEAR OF THE OPENING OF THE LIVERPOOL AND MANCHESTER RAILWAY, 1930.

UNIFORMS

For the first year or two of the LMS period the styles of uniform for the different categories of employees did not change from the pre-group company styles, other than for the issue of LMS buttons with new issues. Not only did the styles vary between the old companies but the periodicity for renewals varied, and the grades of employees who qualified for such heavy outwear as greatcoats, oilskins, and mackintoshes were also different between the companies. Some standardisation was required in styles, in the various garments for each grade, in the staggering of requisitioning orders from each division, and this was introduced progressively.

The LMS clothing factory in Osborne Street, Manchester was the Company's own production unit for new uniforms, and in 1924 almost 100,000 garments were produced — 33,000 jackets, 42,000 trousers, 13,000 vests, 8,800 overcoats, plus a variety of other items. The tallest employee was said to be 6ft. 8in. tall — the smallest a mere 4ft. 3in., and between these two heights there were close on 190,000 employees for whom uniforms were required. Jackets, vests (type of waistcoat) and caps were issued to many grades every year, and trousers were replaced every six months. Overcoats, mackintoshes or capes had a three-year life. Outside contractors were engaged to provide clothing to LMS specifications, and all purchasing, including the cloth and linings for Osborne Street, was done through the Purchasing Section at Euston, where the estimated requirements from each division were collated and orders placed. A clothing store was maintained at St. Rollox, Glasgow, and this serviced the Northern Division of the LMS; Osborne Street, the remaining three divisions, and supplies for the former North Staffordshire section were sent in bulk to Stoke-on-Trent, and those for the Furness and West Cumberland sections, to Barrow-in-Furness, and distribution was arranged from these centres.

Standardisation of grade entitlements and periodicity of issue were completed by mid-1929 with the Goods, Cartage and Dock Grades of employees. Management staff were advised in writing that the grade entitlements must be rigidly enforced, and any employee in the Officemen or Messenger Grades, who did not come into contact with the public as part of their duties, did not qualify for protective outwear unless more than 50 per cent of their time was spent open to the weather.

The first standard LMS uniform issues for four grades who came into contact with the public are shown in the accompanying plates.

Plate 69:

British Railways

Ticket Collector

Stationmaster

Porter

Guard

L. M. & S. R. 135

E.R.O. 40143

ENGINEERING DEPT. WAGES STAFF

SURNAME *Lake*   CHRISTIAN NAMES *George Henry*

SOCIETY............. CLASS.......

DATE OF BIRTH *3. 11. 1909*

SOCIETY............. CLASS.......

no 6336   CLASS............

DATE TO BE EXCEPTED FROM N.U.[*18/9/37*
(where applicable)

MEDICAL EXAM.: DATE...........

WEEKLY DEDUCTIONS FROM WAGES

Date	N.I. H U	L.&N.W. Insurance	L.&N.W. P.&P.	Savings Bank		Rent	P.S.F.	Hospital	P.M.A.	R.B.I.& R.S.O.	Pension Fund Div. B.	Sick Fund Div. B.	Insurance Society Div. B.	Housing Scheme	Total Deductions
4.4.33	9	10													1.7
12.34	9	10					3								1.x
6.1.36	10	10					3								1.11
7.36	10	9					3								1.10
8.9.37	10						3								1.1

PARTICULARS OF SERVICE

Date	Station	No. of Gang	Grade	Class and Area	Remarks	Rate of Wages
4.4.33	*Crewe*	*Ex 3*		*Ind.*	Entered Service *24. 4. 33*	44/.
3.7.33	*Arley*	*190 189*	*Lengthman*	"		44/.
6.8.37						46/.
1.10.37						47/6
11.58						48/.
2.5.88	*Whitacre*	*195*	*Lengthman*	"		48/.
1.7.58						49/.
4.10.39		*Resigned & paid off.*				

WAGES PAID

The system for paying the weekly-paid employees was an interesting, if not unique operation. Wages cards were maintained for all employees and hand-written as the example shows. The cash requirements were analysed for each denomination of note and coin, and advised to the bank. These requirements, when received from the bank, were made up for each employee and the amount placed in a pay-can, bearing a number to correspond with a numbered pay token. At the pay-out, the token was exchanged for the cash amount in the pay-can, and the token was returned to the employee afterwards, ready for use the following week.

The reverse of the wages card recorded any offences committed by the employee and the punishments given, details of any educational awards, grants or allowances given, and details of any accidents to the employee.

Plate 70: Pay-cans — and there were many styles in use, many originating from the pre-group companies.

G. Foxley Collection

Plate 71: A selection of pay tokens.   *G. Foxley Collection*

Plate 72: This type of paper or pamphlet display rack could be found in most stations, and this example originates from a Central Division station, it being identical in size to the standard L&YR issue.

G. Foxley Collection

OUTSIDE CONTRACTORS FOR TRACKWORK

There were a number of private contractors who built trackwork for the LMS and Taylor Bros (Sandiacre) Ltd., was one of them. Using the standard rail and either their own components or those supplied by the railway company, they were contracted to produce specific pointwork layouts and these were prefabricated and laid out in their yard prior to installation. This ensured the various components were of correct size and profile before being transported to the particular location for installation by the LMS permanent way gangs.

Plates 73 & 74: The first view shows a crossover arrangement for Kingmoor, Carlisle, prior to delivery in December, 1942, whilst the second view shows a simple point or switch, built as replacement for a part of the main line in the approach to Southport.

B. C. Lane Collection

Plate 75: Relaying part of St. Pancras Junction with prefabricated pointwork in 1947. The entrance to Somers Town goods depot is seen behind the pall of steam and to the right of the station roof are the Midland Hotel buildings. On the right is the coal depot.

Author's Collection

Plate 76: A view from the roof of St. Pancras Station, showing the interesting approaches to the station. In front of the gasometer is the Midland water tower and engine stabling and to the left and right of the roadway are the coal yards — the curved roof covers the coal drops — and there are two 0-6-0 tank engines occupying the entrances to the Somers Town goods depot.

Author's Collection

TRAINING MOTOR DRIVERS

Plates 77 & 78 (opposite page): The LMS School of Transport at Derby, opened on 22nd July 1938, was portrayed in *LMS Miscellany (Volume II) — Plates 219 & 220,* and it provided training facilities for many different aspects of the LMS operations. These two scenes show a road motor vehicle driver training class in progress, with the instructor using some of the popular Dinky Toy models as a training aid. To create the utmost realism(!) the Carter Paterson van above the instructor's hand has actually broken down — the front wheels have been removed!

National Railway Museum

Equally Famous

The "Flying Scotsman"

The "Golden Arrow"

The "Royal Scot"

The "Cornish Riviera"

THE GENUINE & ORIGINAL

"RAILWAY TEA"

Exclusively blended for and sold only by the undermentioned Institutions and authorised Agents

The GREAT WESTERN STAFF SUPPLY STORES LTD.
The LONDON MIDLAND & SCOTTISH STAFF SUPPLY STORES Ltd.
The LONDON & NORTH-EASTERN STAFF SUPPLY STORES Ltd.
The SOUTHERN STAFF SUPPLY STORES Ltd.

WARNING—You will be quite certain of obtaining the genuine Railway Tea if you look for our Names and Trade Mark which appear on every packet of Tea.

LIBERAL COMMISSION.
Application for Agencies should be addressed to Head Office:
18, Sheldon Street, London, W.2.

Plate 79: 'Royal Scot Tea'.

Plate 80: A simple paper sticky label, used for sealing re-used envelopes and similar paperwork.

Author's Collection

IF UNDELIVERED
please return to
L. M. S. Railway
ST. ENOCH STN,
GLASGOW

LMS	E.R.O. 21502	No. OF PACK-AGES	No. OF PASSENGERS		DL
EXCESS CHARGES { TO PAY_____			FIRST	THIRD	
PAID _____					
DELIVERED LUGGAGE					
FROM_____					
TO _____					

Plate 82: A small coloured poster issued to advertise the 'Removal Service', and the 'Luggage in Advance' Service.

M. Brooks Collection

Plate 81: Another feature of the School of Transport at Derby was the central hall with complete working model railway, fully fitted for authentic operation. The floor of the hall was at a lower level than the side walkways.

J. Miller Collection

ADVERTISING TICKET INSETS

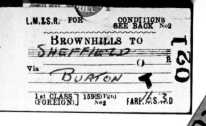

Plates 83 & 84: In 1930, the LMS placed a contract with a private company, Insets Ltd., for the supply of 200 million tickets per year to a patented design which provided for a display advertising insert to be slotted into the centre of the ticket, rather like the filling in a sandwich. It was estimated that the revenue generated from the advertising inserts would cover the cost of the ticket printing, thereby reducing the cost of providing tickets for passengers considerably. In addition to mainland LMS services, Insets' tickets were also used on the related LMS lines in Northern Ireland where the tickets were normally provided by the LMS.

Whilst one of this type was illustrated in *LMS Miscellany (Volume I)*, further examples here show the inset tucked inside the ticket, and partly withdrawn. The two panels of advertising insets show both sides of a selection of twenty five, and there were a variety of others (the BDV and JCQO are misplaced in the lower panel). One example even offered a free bottle of wine — Burgoyne's port-type wine.

G. Waite Collection

RAILWAY SERVANTS' ORPHANAGE

The Derby Orphanage was established in 1875 by railwaymen, and a small cottage on London Road, Derby was rented to provide a home for the first eleven children. The work of the Orphanage increased and larger premises were required and found on Ashbourne Road and, by 1924, there were 272 children residents, between the ages of 6 and 15. From 1881, when the Derby Orphanage became allied with the Railway Benevolent Institution, funds to sustain the work and provide for extensions and other requirements were raised through various charity appeals, festivals, and by voluntary donations from the public and the railway employees.

At Crewe, the Webb Orphanage fulfilled a similar role with buildings set in more than 5 acres of ground and all facilities.

The children received a full education in the normal town schools and, whilst gymnasium facilities, workshops and sports equipment were provided, the girls were given training in a variety of home-care pursuits — cookery, laundry, sewing and dressmaking, and examinations to test the progress were held every year.

Plate 85: One of the many collecting boxes for Orphanage funds. Children pestered parents and grandparents for the coin which would make the wheels turn on the encased model, once it had been dropped in the slot. These were a favourite with children and adults alike, as were the donation boxes attached to the 'Collecting Dogs' at the major stations — *see LMS Miscellany (Volume II) — Plate 5.*

Author's Collection

Plate 86: The Webb Orphanage at Crewe.

Author's Collection

Plate 87: The Centenary Medal issued in 1938 to commemorate the 100th Anniversary of the opening of the London & Birmingham Railway in 1838. The obverse has the Euston arch, and beneath are the names of the Chairman, Engineer and Architect — George Carr Glyn, — Robert Stephenson, and Philip Hardwicke. The reverse has the names of the LMS Directors and Secretary, headed by Lord Stamp, Chairman.

S. G. Underwood Collection

THE TRIUMPH OF 'THE ROYAL SCOT'

This title was used for a booklet issued by the Company as a postscript to the successful tour of North America by 'The Royal Scot' in 1933. *Plates 39 to 42 in LMS Miscellany (Volume I),* show the engine being prepared at Crewe Works in readiness for shipment on board the Canadian Pacific Steamship *Beaverdale* from Tilbury docks to Montreal. Loading began on 5th April 1933, and arrival in Montreal was on the 21st April, and after unloading, running trials were successfully completed on 30th April, a top speed of 75m.p.h. being achieved on the initial trip on foreign soil. The centrepiece of the tour was the 'Century of Progress' Exposition in Chicago, held from 25th May to 10th October, during which 'The Royal Scot' and its train of eight coaches stood alongside 'The Burlington' train. After exhibition on 1st May at the Windsor Station, Montreal, when 18,500 people viewed the train, it left for Cincinnati, via Ottawa, Niagara, New York and Washington, with exhibition stops in most towns en route.

The 303 mile journey to the Chicago site was the last working before the Exposition period, and such was the interest created by 'The Royal Scot train', that a post-Exposition tour to the west coast of the United States was quickly arranged. Los Angeles, San Francisco, Vancouver, Calgary, Winnipeg, Chicago, London were visited prior to return to Montreal, and shipment from there to London, England by the *S.S. Beaverdale,* leaving on 24th November.

The train travelled 11,194 miles under her own steam, and was inspected by 3,021,601 visitors, of whom 2,074,348 passed through the train during the 'Century of Progress' Exposition. More than eighty cities and towns played host to the visitors from Great Britain.

The transatlantic journey was borne out of a visit to America in 1930 of the LMS Chairman and President, Sir Joseph Stamp, GBE, and 'The Royal Scot' train was the only British exhibit at the Chicago Exposition. Its normal route, linking England and Scotland, created a much wider sphere of interest.

The locomotive for the tour — No. 6100 — was not the original No. 6100 *Royal Scot* built in 1927 by the North British Locomotive Company, Glasgow, but a later Derby-built engine which was believed to be No. 6152 as the one which exchanged identities.

Upon its return to Britian the train steamed into a decorated Euston Station, at noon on 15th December 1933, with its bell clanking to officially bring the tour to a close.

A welcoming party headed by Sir Josiah Stamp, greeted the arrival, and a band of Scottish pipers from the LMS 21st Glasgow Scouts and Rovers provided appropriate musical accompaniment. His Majesty King George VI sent a message of congratulations which was read by Sir Josiah, and the President then presented inscribed gold watches to the crew and staff who had been with the train. During the following three days, 33,600 people inspected the complete train.

The locomotive was fitted with a commemorative plaque beneath each nameplate, and the train then visited various parts of the system and was open to public exhibition. Before being returned to service, the headlight was removed, but the bell remained.

The tour was a great success for the Company and every bit of publicity was captured in the months following its return to LMS territory.

Copies of the booklet *The Triumph of the Royal Scot* are now collectors' items and a great number of those issued appear to have been autographed by Driver W. Gilbertson, Fireman J. Jackson, both of Carlisle, and Fitter C. Woods of Crewe, all of whom were with the train throughout the tour, and by Fireman T. Blackett of Carlisle, who joined the tour party as relief engineman for the post-Exposition tour. Tributes flowed from many directions.

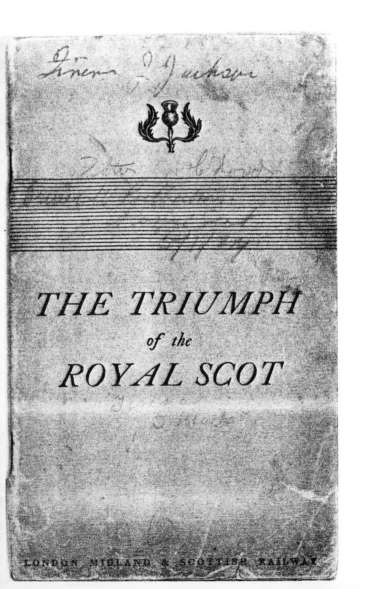

THE ROYAL SCOT

SOME TRIBUTES

"The riding of The Royal Scot is perfect. I have been much impressed with its comfort and particularly with the smooth starting and stopping."—*Mr. Rufus Dawes,*
Chairman of the Exposition

* * *

"The visit of The Royal Scot to America has explained to the people of the United States and Canada some idea of England's efficiency and greatness. Viewing The Royal Scot—small, but solid and efficient—is just like getting an insight into the genius of the British race."—*"The Vancouver Sun"*

* * *

"I have been much impressed with the workmanship of the train which provides a lesson for American railroads."
—*General Craig.*

* * *

"I congratulate your Company on the fact that The Royal Scot has become an ambassadorial train of inestimable value."
—*Mr. B. G. D. Phillip,*
Chairman, Foreign Trade Bureau, Vancouver

* * *

Plate 88: The autographed cover of the booklet given to those who inspected the train after its return to Great Britain — this copy was signed on 5th January 1934.

Author's Collection

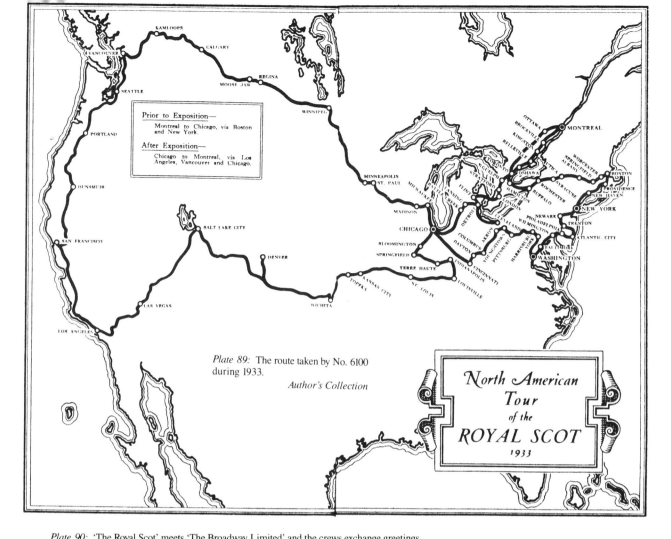

Prior to Exposition—
Montreal to Chicago, via Boston and New York.

After Exposition—
Chicago to Montreal, via Los Angeles, Vancouver and Chicago.

Plate 89: The route taken by No. 6100 during 1933.

Author's Collection

North American Tour of the **ROYAL SCOT** *1933*

Plate 90: 'The Royal Scot' meets 'The Broadway Limited' and the crews exchange greetings. There appears to be a microphone on a tripod between the tracks, possibly for speeches to be made. These two trains ran alongside one another for a short distance.

Author's Collection

Giants of Speed and Power at A Century of Progress.

The Royal Scot
Famous London-Glasgow-Edinburgh flyer of the London, Midland & Scottish Ry.
1st class corridor brake coach
1st class sleeper coach
3rd class sleeper coach
Lounge car and brake
1st class corridor vestibule coach
Electric kitchen car
3rd class vestibule coach
3rd class corridor brake coach

The Burlington Train
A composite train made up of equipment from regular Burlington trains.
U. S. Railway Post Office car
Reclining chair car (Aristocrat)
Dining car (Black Hawk)
Salon-bed room Pullman (Black Hawk)
14 Section Pullman (Aristocrat)
Lounge car (Ak-Sar-Ben)

The Pride of the Prairies
Engine 35 . . . vintage of 1882. Behind it is a reproduction of the first railway car in which U. S. Mail was assorted in transit, (1862) and thus the actual starting point of today's extensive Railway Post Office service.

Plate 91: The official postcard souvenir of the 'Century of Progress', with a note on the reverse' for mailing in the postal car on the Burlington's World's Fair Exhibition Train. The train consisted of a selection of LMS carriage types rather than the impression given that it was 'The Royal Scot' train.

Gavin Wilson Collection

Plate 92 (below): The train at Albany, USA on the New York Central system, soon after arriving on American soil.

Gavin Wilson Collection

Plate 93: Fold-out pamphlets were given out to visitors to the Chicago Exposition, showing the places and distances of the Euston to Glasgow and Edinburgh routes, and many of the beauty spots in Scotland, with the centrepiece the Company's world-famous Gleneagles Hotel. A Bassett-Lowke model of 'The Royal Scot' engine and eight coach train was used as background to the route distances. This is an illustration of the cover.

Author's Collection

Plate 94: No. 6100 stands in the yard at Crewe North Shed on 20th August 1939 awaiting the next turn of duty. The plaque is shown beneath the nameplate, and a Stanier curved side tender has replaced the earlier Stanier straight-sided tender which accompanied the engine to America.

N. R. E. Williams

Plate 95: Here the tour train is seen at Llandudno during its exhibition tour. The commemorative
plates are seen below the side nameplate.

British Railways

ROYAL SCOT ON EXHIBITION

Plate 96: Long before the North American tour, 'The Royal Scot' was displayed at a number of
locations to the public and here the banners announce its presence at Birmingham (New Street) Station
in 1927.

British Railways

E.R.O. 21556/11

L M S

BIRMINGHAM

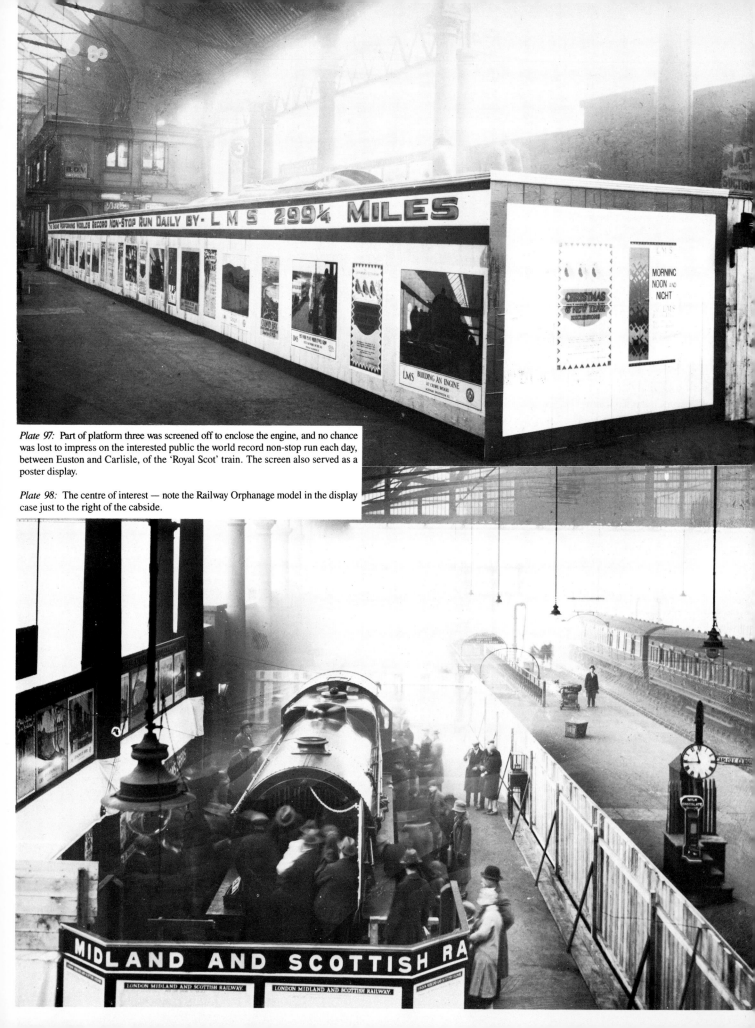

Plate 97: Part of platform three was screened off to enclose the engine, and no chance was lost to impress on the interested public the world record non-stop run each day, between Euston and Carlisle, of the 'Royal Scot' train. The screen also served as a poster display.

Plate 98: The centre of interest — note the Railway Orphanage model in the display case just to the right of the cabside.

THE LMS IN NORTH AMERICA

A joint British railways' office was based in New York with each British company having its own representatives. The LMS provided passenger and freight representatives in New York, and a representative for both classes of traffic in Los Angeles, and also Montreal, Canada. LMS agents were also appointed in all major towns and cities, with the larger cities having a number of appointed agents. There were at least 39 in New York City, in addition to the joint office.

Tourist traffic from America to Britain was the major objective, and publicity material was specially printed for distribution through the North American offices and agents. Folded maps were the major give-away, and these carried a map of the LMS system, with subsidiary connecting lines (the GWR, SR, & LNER) also shown. On the reverse were timetables for the principal routes, together with information on the LMS hotels, places of interest, and general information on availability of tickets, luncheon baskets, etc.

Through merchandise traffic was also booked through the North American agents.

Plate 99: The outer covers of three maps are shown in this photograph — the 1929, 1930 and 1932 issues. Note the 1929 example has a note regarding London and Liverpool — the two major transatlantic ports connected to the LMS system.

M. Brooks Collection

TELEPHONE
Gramercy 2931

CABLE ADDRESS
"Norwestern, Newyork"

LONDON, MIDLAND & SCOTTISH RAILWAY
OF GREAT BRITAIN
OFFICE OF THE GENERAL PASSENGER AND FREIGHT AGENT
200 FIFTH AVENUE

REFERENCE TO YOUR

PLEASE REFER TO

JOHN FAIRMAN
GENERAL PASSENGER AND FREIGHT AGENT

NEW YORK.

Plate 100: The Company's letterheading for the New York representative.

M. Brooks Collection

PASSENGER STATION DETAIL

The accompanying table gives details of the largest passenger stations owned by the Company and, of course, it is a well-known fact that the longest railway platform in Great Britain was the one which linked the Victoria and Exchange Stations in Manchester, at 2,194ft. Station photographs are always of interest to the railway modeller as well as to the enthusiast, and it is when we look at these bygone scenes, that we realise so much of the traditional railway scenario has been lost forever. Modellers look for details so that they can enhance and improve the miniature scenes they create, and to achieve as near the prototypical authenticity as possible. The following plates are full of such details.

L. M. S.—LARGEST PASSENGER STATIONS.

Station.	Section.	Total Platform Lines.	Area occupied.	Length of longest Platform.	Total length of Platforms.
			Acres.	Feet.	Feet.
Barking	L. T. S.	8	4	760	5,904
Birmingham (New Street)	L. N. W. & Mid. ...	15	14	770	8,550
Blackpool (North) ...	L. & Y. & L. N. W.	15	13¾	760	9,900
Blackpool (Central) ...	L. & Y. & L. N. W.	14	10	840	9,030
Carlisle (Citadel)	Cal. & L. N. W. ...	8	15	1,422	6,987
Chester (Joint)	L. N. W. & G. W.	11	10	1,340	7,307
Crewe	L. N. W.	16	23	1,509	11,394
Derby	Mid.	6	5½	1,146	5,796
Liverpool (Exchange) ...	L. & Y.	10	10¾	704	6,406
Liverpool (Lime Street) ...	L. N. W.	11	10	690	7,157
London (Euston)	L. N. W.	15	18	1,030	10,776
London (St. Pancras)* ...	Mid.	7	9	829	5,109
London (Broad Street) ...	N. L.	9	3	730	4,867
Manchester (Victoria and Exchange)	L. & Y. & L. N. W.	21	23	†2,194	13,947
Nottingham	Mid.	6	9	1,177	5,974
Preston	L. N. W. & L. & Y.	15	10½	1,253	10,102
Rugby	L. N. W.	8	9	1,415	5,478
Sheffield	Mid.	9	15	1,313	7,880
Southend	L. T. S.	6	3½	926	4,657
Southport (Chapel Street)	L. & Y.	13	14¾	1,138	9,324
Tilbury	L. T. S.	6	4½	878	4,102
Willesden	Main Line ...	8	7	1,210	6,234
	New Station ...	4	2	405	1,410
	High Level ...	2	2	618	1,233
		14	11	2,233	8,877
SCOTLAND—					
Aberdeen (Joint) ...	Cal. & G. N. of S.	13	11½	1,596	11,340
Glasgow (Central) ...	Cal.	13	13	1,040	9,080
Glasgow (Low Level) ...	Cal.	4	2	675	2,245
Glasgow (St. Enoch) ...	G. & S. W. ...	12	13½	1,128	9,561

* St. Pancras is the largest Station in Great Britain under a single span roof.
† Connecting Platform, Victoria and Exchange, 2,194 feet, is the longest platform in Great Britain.

Plate 101: In addition to the longest platform, having the largest station under a single span roof, and a host of other unique features, an LMS station on the Isle of Anglesey could claim that it had the longest station name in the world — LLANFAIRPWLLGWYNGYLLGOGERYCHWYRNDROBWLLLL-ANTYSILIOGOGOGOCH — 58 letters . . . and often referred to as Llanfair P.G. Translated, the name reads 'The Church of St. Mary in a hollow of white hazel, near to a rapid whirlpool and to St. Tysilio's Church near to a red cave'. The station was a tourist attraction and there were several different nameboards used during the LMS period, all of non-standard LMS design. The ex L&NWR station seat has Llanfair on the back rail.

N. R. E. Williams

WHITENING PLATFORM EDGES

Plate 102: The white line on the edge of station platforms was said to be provided to prevent passengers from approaching too close to the edge in foggy weather — some fog! It also served a similar purpose during wartime black-out conditions where artificial lighting was greatly subdued. In this photograph the porter has a plank with steel bars which hooks over the platform edge to ensure a uniform width and straight edge is maintained. In 1925, the LMS workshops built a number of machines which were capable of marking a solid white line at an average speed of 65yds. per minute, and these could even be used whilst trains were at the same platform.

National Railway Museum

Plate 103: Platform 'clutter' at Leamington Spa (Avenue) Station in 1937. Note the Southern Railway poster board 100 miles or so from Southern territory.

G. Coltas

$\left(\frac{46}{861}\right)$ **LONDON MIDLAND AND SCOTTISH RAILWAY COMPANY.**

EDINBURGH STATION.

LEFT LUGGAGE DEPOT.

*Date,*_____19___

*Ticket No.*_____

*No. of Articles,*_____

Plate 104: Liverpool (Exchange) in the early part of 1928. The enquiry office roof is interesting, showing the glass **roof** surrounded by advertising panels. Note too the handbill display, the variety of posters, the ticket barriers, and the central roadway which was a feature at most of the large stations.

Author's Collection

Plate 105: Ex-Midland Railway platform trolleys, types 200 and 201, parked at the end of one of the St. Pancras platforms. The fire buckets show up well in this view.

G. Coltas

London Midland and Scottish Railway Company
(CALEDONIAN SECTION)

(46/856)

ST. PANCRAS

FROM

KIRRIEMUIR

Plate 107 (opposite): Sheffield (Midland) Station is one which retains many of its original features to this day. Although this 1905 view is pre-LMS period, it contains a great deal of interest for the railway modeller and historian, and there would have been few changes to this scene between 1905 and when the LMS took over in 1923. The wide platforms covered by cantelevered awnings, a multiplicity of signboards, and a well-stocked bookstall, the panelled bridgework, and at the far end of the platform, a wide stairway leading to platforms 2 to 9, are all features of interest.

V. R. Anderson Collection

Plate 106: One of the ornate London & Birmingham Railway station buildings at Bletchley.

Author's Collection

Plate 108 (opposite): Squires Gate Station opened on 14th September 1931, on the Blackpool borough boundary and close to the airstrip, which was later destined to become one of the airports served by Railway Air Services Ltd., partly owned by the LMS. It was perhaps the nearest LMS station to serve the Company's air services when, in April 1935, a new service from Liverpool to the Isle of Man called at Squires Gate airport. There were comparatively few truly LMS-built stations, for the vast majority had been inherited from the pre-1923 companies, but Squires Gate was an LMS-designed and built station. Interestingly, the posters on the left-hand shop front, behind the men, invitingly portray other resorts for holidays, with Scotland and the Company's Gleneagles Hotel, the Sunny South, or the Lake District, all featured. Note the two sizes and patterns of posterboard, and District Bank tenancy!

British Railways

Plate 109 (opposite): The platform level looking towards Blackpool (Central). Note the station name painted on the rustic seat. This type of cast-iron seat was used by the Midland Railway, and it is interesting to note that there are a number of these on this new Western Division station, rather than the former L&NWR wrought ironwork type.

British Railways

Plate 110: The LM&S initials cast into the wrought-iron platform screen at Llandudno Station.

J. Miller

| LMS | E.R.O. 21556/13 |
| | O.P. 3 |

BLACKPOOL

(CENTRAL)

| LONDON MIDLAND AND SCOTTISH RAILWAY COMPANY. | E. F. 70. |
| | R 2a. |

Newcastle-on-Tyne

Plate 111: Add a seasonal touch to your station scene . . .

Author's Collection

WITHOUT CATCHING COLD —

LONDON MIDLAND AND SCOTTISH RAILWAY

The *Best Way* TO SEND YOUR

Christmas Parcels IS BY

LMS

PROMPT COLLECTION   QUICK TRANSIT
EARLY DELIVERY

Plate 112: Another station in Anglesey — Valley, 3½ miles from the ferry port of Holyhead. The nameboard is let into the goods shed wall. Note the platform edging and the blue drain bricks used for the platform.

British Railways

Plate 113: The image was well-kept and tidy stations — a daily chore for the porter.

Author's Collection

London Midland and Scottish Railway Coy
(Glasgow and South Western Section.)

JOHNSTONE

Plate 114: An unusual visitor to Tean Station trackwork!

J. Miller

Plate 115: GENTLEMEN, at your convenience! A Walter Macparlane & Co, Glasgow cast-iron 'gents' at St. Albans City in 1945. Note too the advertisement boards for Ryder's seeds fitted to the lamp posts on both platforms. Well-known firms often used the railway station or lineside for advertising their 'home town' presence.

Author's Collection

Plate 116: This is the ticket office and entrance gates to Derby (Midlands) Station used for excursion train traffic, formerly designated the Midland Railway 3rd class booking office. The former first class booking office had been redesignated for first and third class ordinary ticket holders.

Plate 117: A regular chore, refilling the handbill rack at Hatch End Station, and judging by the variety of excursions and cheap ticket offers, bargains for all. A restaurant car excursion to the steeplechasing at Derby; a Wolverhampton Wanderers v Arsenal 1st Division soccer match; bright and breezy Blackpool with a choice of January, February or March; and one handbill advertising the hire of LMS lantern slide lecture evenings with a choice of 32 subjects. The date would appear to be in late 1937. There are several bills for regular day, half-day and evening excursion venues operative from October 1937, and the football matches advertised are in the early weeks of 1938 — five matches advertised.

British Railways

(H.R.)
(A. 474)
LONDON MIDLAND AND SCOTTISH RAILWAY COMPANY.
(HIGHLAND SECTION).

LUGGAGE.

From

TO EUSTON

Via Dunkeld, Cal. and Carlisle.

Plate 118: The same employee now turns his hand to the poster boards at Hatch End.

British Railways

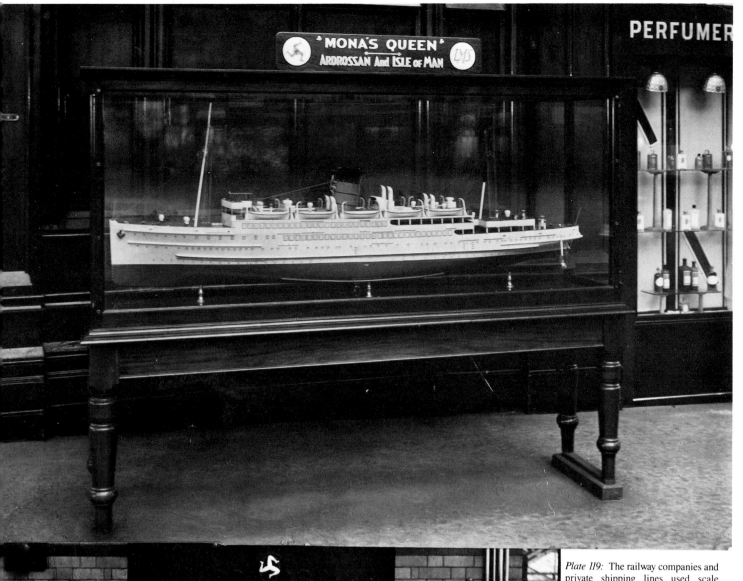

'MONA'S QUEEN'
ARDROSSAN And ISLE OF MAN

PERFUMER

EXPRESS TRAIN & STEAMER SERVICES TO ISLE OF MAN

EVERY WEEKDAY
LIVERPOOL & DOUGLAS THROUGHOUT YEAR
FLEETWOOD & DOUGLAS DURING SEASON
DAY EXCURSIONS FROM BOLTON TO DOUGLAS VIA FLEETWOOD
WEEKDAYS DURING SEASON

Plate 119: The railway companies and private shipping lines used scale models of their vessels in show cases to advertise services. *Mona's Queen* is shown here at Wolverhampton LMS station.

Isle of Man Steam Packet Company

Plate 120: King Orry III is seen here at Bolton Station. Other models were to be seen at major stations, where they would best service the interests of the steamership company.

Isle of Man Steam Packet Company

LAND OWNERSHIP

Total land acreage occupied by the London, Midland & Scottish Railway Company throughout the kingdom was collosal and ran into many thousands. Taking 1935 as the mid-point of the LMS period, the following mileages of lines gives an indication of the area of land occupied:

	m. ch.
Main and Principal lines owned by the Company	2,932.34
Minor and Branch lines owned by the Company	3,801.00
Jointly owned lines (LMS share)	178.72
Leased or worked	3.25
	6,915.51

Split as to:

Single lines	2,307.24
Double lines	3,803.19
With more than two lines	805.08
	6,915.51

With lines reduced to single track length:

Running lines	13,366.17
Sidings	6,015.49
	19,381.66

All the mileage was standard gauge, except the 8 miles 21 chains 2ft. 6in. gauge section of the Leek & Manifold Light Railway in Staffordshire.

In addition to the land ownership occupied by running lines, a great deal of land was occupied by offices, stations, goods yards, works and enquiry offices in towns, although many of these were only on lease.

Plate 122: For every plot of land, whether large or small, and many were just so, paper documents were required to maintain evidence of legal ownership, and to quantify the tonnage of paper so retained would be impossible. This legal Agreement covers the widening and improvement of the highway near Laindon Station in Essex, and all legal documents were held in strongroom accommodation, referred to by the LMS Estates Department as the 'Muniment Room' — a room for keeping the records, charters, seals, deeds and the like.

Plate 121: Ex-Midland Railway houses in Midland Road, Bradford, now nicely restored and set for many future years of occupation — April, 1985. Note the diagonal palings.

J. Hinchcliffe

In addition to the 'railway land', the LMS also owned land and property which did not form part of the railway or stations, and there were 9,065 acres of agricultural land, and some 2,230 acres of urban and surburban land (1935), the bulk of which brought in rental income. A total of 23,946 houses were also owned and let as follows:

Labouring class dwellings	1,330
Houses and cottages for Company's servants	12,125
Other houses and cottages	10,491
Total	23,946(1935)

Rental income from houses and lands amounted to £857,795 in 1935, all of which contributed to make the LMS one of the largest landowners in the United Kingdom.

Many of the houses were in terraces close to stations, engine sheds and goods yards and let to railway employees, whilst the stationmasters either lived in the station buildings, or in an adjacent dwelling.

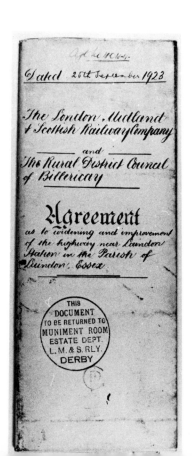

Plate 123: Two cast-iron signs, typical of many put up around the LMS territory (*see also Page 63*):

Author's Collection

Plate 124: A 'Sites for Factories' poster used extensively to advertise the land adjacent to the railway lines which the LMS owned, and would make available for new factory development. Where siding connections were provided, part of the agreement was that all goods not sold in the local area would be consigned by rail.
National Railway Museum

CIGARETTE CARDS

Plate 125: The Company's engines and some of the day-to-day activities were used as subject matter for cigarette cards issued by all the major 'fag' manufacturers, and they were eagerly collected by adults and children. The majority were in full colour which added to the attraction for collectors, and these are but a minute selection of the many cards which still circulate in collectors' circles today.

G. Norman Collection

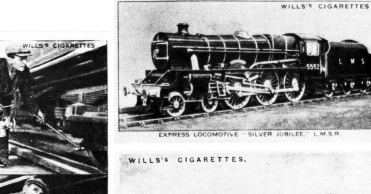

LMS DIVERS

This was another unusual occupation at first sight, but perhaps not so surprising when one remembers that the LMS owned a number of port areas and docks, and a fleet of sea-going ships, to say nothing of the steamer fleet on Lake Windermere. Barrow was the principal centre for the Company's diving operations, and divers were usually recruited from shipyards, shipwrights having experience in working with a variety of materials and crafts, and a knowledge of boat-building trades.

A small diving bell was also owned by the LMS. In addition to work for the Company, the diving gear and men were available for hire by local authorities in connection with the laying of underwater cables, gas and water mains, and for reservoir inspection work, whilst private firms required their services in connection with shipbuilding and launching work, to ensure there were no underwater obstructions impeding a vessel's passage down the slipway.

The limit to which the LMS men could work was 100ft. down, but normal operations were in much shallower waters.

L. M. & S. R.
Barrow

Plates 126 & 127: LMS divers in the water.

Author's Collection

Plate 128 (opposite upper): The calendar driers and ironing machines. The heated rollers can be seen on the right-hand machine and the laundresses are folding the pieces as they come off and stacking them in the trollies ready for despatch.

Author's Collection

The Willesden laundry provided more than four million pieces each year, and when the laundries elsewhere on the system and those attached to the Company's hotels were considered, the LMS laundry service was a multi-million-piece operation.

LMS LAUNDRIES

There were nine of these laundries around the system, but the largest was located at Willesden Junction, approximately six miles from Euston. Thirty three staff were employed at the laundry, one foreman, six laundrymen, and twenty six laundresses, and they were responsible for all linen from the Euston Hotel, several refreshment rooms, and the sleeping and dining cars operating on the Western Division. It was an operation geared to coping with vast quantities in a short space of time, and was equipped with the most modern machinery and equipment available.

Soiled linen was brought in by motor van and placed into cylindrical washing machines for a thorough cleansing. A centrifugal drier or a hydro extractor was used to damp-dry the articles in much the same way as a tumble drier works today, except that those which the LMS used were of considerable size and capacity. Drying and airing was another rapid process, with the linen passing through a continuous calendar drier, consisting of heated rollers covered with an absorbent material which removed the remaining moisture, eventually being removed and packed for use again. Certain articles were hand-pressed before re-use.

A machine for starching collars and shirt fronts was also part of the equipment, and these items were 'glossed' during the ironing process.

In 1938, a new laundry was opened at Hunslet, Leeds, on land which had previously served as a stable block, and this was for servicing the Company hotels in Bradford, the Midland Hotel, and the Queens Hotel in Leeds, which had opened following rebuilding in 1937, as well as providing linen for services starting from these two cities.

Plate 129 (opposite lower): The washing room at Willesden laundry, a 1939 view.

Author's Collection

E.R.O. 21556/86

L M S

LEEDS

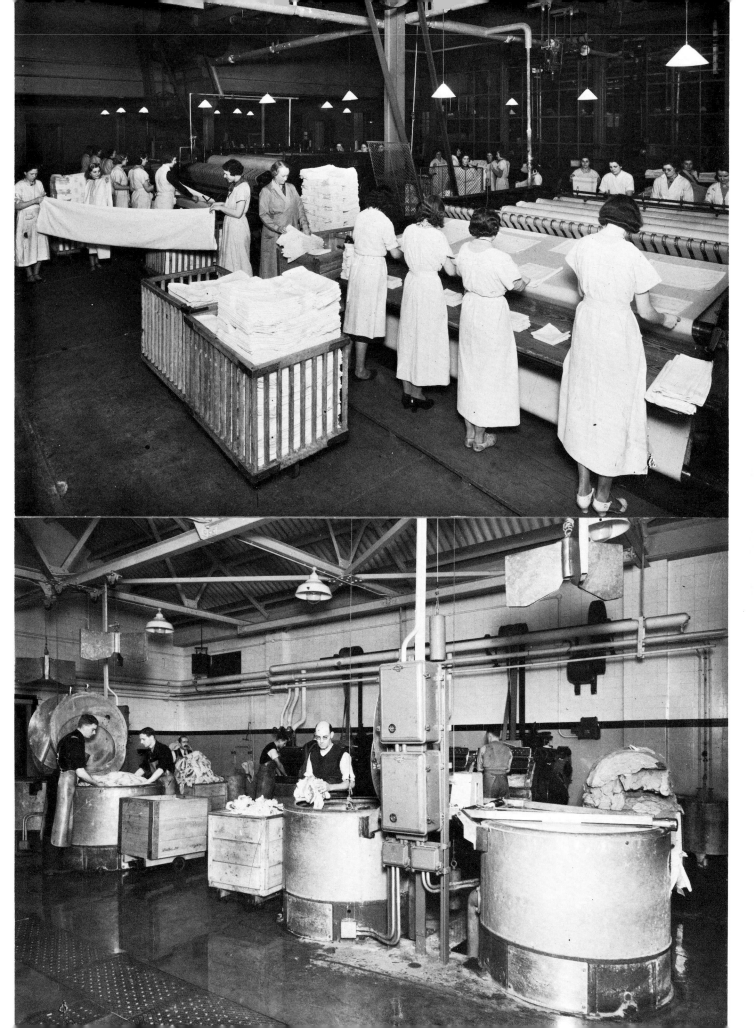

CARRIAGE PICTURES

Plates 130 & 131 (opposite page): Compartment interiors were used for advertising some LMS services, and to display photographs or paintings of locations which could be reached by travelling on the Company's trains. A wide variety of places were featured, and now such pictures are a favourite subject with collectors of railway memorabilia. Interiors of cathedrals, landscape and seascape scenes were popular, and the sight of a crowded Blackpool promenade could well have influenced the destination of next year's holiday — either against going, or the desire to be part of it!

G. Foxley Collection

ST. NINIAN'S CATHEDRAL, PERTH (INTERIOR).

STAY AT LMS HOTELS

AYR: STATION HOTEL

BIRMINGHAM: QUEEN'S HOTEL

*BRADFORD: MIDLAND HOTEL

*DERBY: MIDLAND HOTEL

DORNOCH: DORNOCH HOTEL (Open May to September.)

EDINBURGH: CALEDONIAN HOTEL

FURNESS ABBEY: FURNESS ABBEY HOTEL

LONDON: EUSTON HOTEL

GLASGOW: CENTRAL HOTEL / ST. ENOCH HOTEL

GLENEAGLES: GLENEAGLES HOTEL (Open Easter to November.)

HOLYHEAD: STATION HOTEL

INVERNESS: STATION HOTEL

KYLE OF LOCHALSH: LOCHALSH HOTEL

*LEEDS: QUEEN'S HOTEL

LIVERPOOL: *ADELPHI / EXCHANGE HOTEL

*MANCHESTER: MIDLAND HOTEL

*MORECAMBE: MIDLAND HOTEL

PRESTON: PARK HOTEL

*STOKE-ON-TRENT: NORTH STAFFORD HOTEL

STRATFORD-UPON-AVON: WELCOMBE HOTEL

STRATHPEFFER: HIGHLAND HOTEL (Open May to September.)

TURNBERRY: TURNBERRY HOTEL

Also at Belfast, Crewe, Dumfries, Larne, Portrush, and at Greenore in association with the G.N. of I. Rly.

* TELEGRAMS: "MIDOTEL"   TELEGRAMS: "BESTOTEL"

E.R.O. 53503.

KYLE OF LOCHALSH.   ROSS-SHIRE.

RAILWAY ARCHITECTURE   WOLVERTON VIADUCT

BLACKPOOL   LANCASHIRE

PITTVILLE GARDENS · CHELTENHAM

THE WEST COAST 'ROAD' ROUTE

Following the opening of the Mersey Tunnel by King George V on the 18th July 1934, the LMS Hotel Services issued this pamphlet detailing a 'road' route from London to two of its prestigious hotels in Scotland, the Gleneagles Hotel and the Turnberry Hotel.

The new 'West Coast Route' by road took in Banbury, Stratford-on-Avon, Chester, 'the new Mersey Tunnel', Liverpool, Preston, Kendal, and Carlisle, and thence north to either Gleneagles or Turnberry. In addition to a note of the LMS hotels on this route, a brief resumé of the towns through which it passed was also given.

The LMS anticipated the new tunnel would be of considerable interest to travellers, particularly those with motor cars. It was described as the greatest achievement of modern engineering, and with its three mile length — entrance to entrance —, with a total tunnel length including branch tunnels of 2.87 miles, it is still the longest road tunnel in Great Britain.

Shortly after issue a small insert to match the pamphlet was added, to give details of the daily rail services between Euston and Gleneagles.

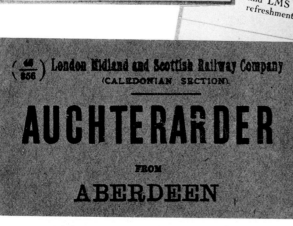

Plate 132   *Author's Collection*

THE WORLD FAMOUS GLENEAGLES HOTEL — LMS

Gleneagles Hotel was the Company's most prestigious hotel and world famous for both its cuisine and the golf courses surrounding it — indeed, even in 1985, it continues to enjoy a world-wide reputation for excellence, and the LMS can take great credit for building it, after taking the land over from the Caledonian Railway at the Grouping. The accompanying photographs show examples of brochures published for the hotel and, in one, the following is written: 'There is no holiday resort in the world that has a higher reputation than Gleneagles Hotel, yet it was only opened as recently as 5th June 1924. There must be something altogether outstanding about the hotel, its surroundings and facilities, to have brought it to such a position of pre-eminence in so short a period.'

In addition to the normal tariff, which ranged up to £4 per day for a suite for two persons, special golf weekends, leaving London on Friday night and **returning Monday night**, were advertised for £12.15s. first class and £9 third class, including private bathroom. Golf, tennis, swimming, riding, dancing, shooting and billiards were available at what was described as 'The Northern Outpost of Luxury — Supreme for Glorious Holidays'.

Plates 133 & 134 opposite

Author's Collection

Gleneagles
Hotel Perthshire

MAIN ENTRANCE AND DRIVE

Aerial View
GLENEAGLES HOTEL

GLORIOUS GLENEAGLES

SWIMMING BATH

GLEN
HOTEL
EAGLES

The Dining Room
Gleneagles Hotel

Page Eleven

Plate 135: In one Gleneagles brochure
was a page of commercial advertising
— does it surprise you to know that the
'ketchup' was made in Canada!

Author's Collection

WHEN YOU STAY AT
GLENEAGLES
HOTEL

you expect to be served with the best of foods and the
best of condiments.
So, too, when you stay at any L.M.S. Hotel.
No wonder then you always find

HEINZ TOMATO KETCHUP

on the tables — the Ketchup that is made in Canada
from sun-ripened tomatoes, picked, cooked and bottled
all in a day. What a difference it makes even to the best
of cold meats, fish steak, chops.

ONE OF THE

HEINZ
57
VARIETIES

THER VARIETIES—MADE IN LONDON
nz Baked Beans   Heinz Salad Cream

Page Thirty-one

GRADIENTS ON THE LMS

The steepest mainline gradient in Great Britain was the 2 mile 5 chain Lickey Incline between Bromsgrove and Blackwell, on the Bristol to Birmingham line, with a rise of 1 in 37½ in the 'up' direction — the Bristol line was the only main line on the LMS in which the 'up' and 'down' directions corresponded to north and south respectively. On all other lines the 'up' direction was southerly.

The Lickey Incline commenced at the northern end of Bromsgrove Station and all trains were required to stop and take on banking support, and for this purpose the Midland had built an 0-10-0 locomotive of massive proportions which quickly became known as the 'Lickey Banker'. In addition, a number of 0-6-0 tank engines were also allocated to Bromsgrove Shed, and these worked in twos and threes, or a pair with the banker for the heaviest of expresses.

Beattock Bank on the West Coast Main Line, between Carlisle and Glasgow, was another steep incline over 10 miles long, rising in parts at 1 in 69 to 1 in 88 between Beattock and Beattock Summit, and banking engines were added to the rear of all but the lightest trains. South of Carlisle the famous Shap Summit was another point at which banking support was required, and for this purpose Tebay Shed had an allocation of tank engines.

The steepest gradients however, were those on the goods only Cromford and High Peak line in Derbyshire, with a 1 in 8 climb on Sheep Pasture incline worked by a stationary steam engine. On the same railway, the Hopton Incline, 1 in 14 for 5 chains, was worked by tank engines using as much power as they could to storm the bank, and the surrounding countryside echoed to the pounding exhaust sounds.

The accompanying table lists the steepest gradients on the LMS and there is also a table showing the highest altitudes on the system. Wanlockhead Station, terminus of the former Caledonian branch from Elvanfoot, between Carlisle and Carstairs, was the highest station in Great Britain at 1,412ft. above sea level — it is perhaps surprising that none of the stations in the Highlands area further north could take this title.

Loading of trains over steeply-graded sections was closely controlled, and each locomotive power classification was subject to maximum loadings, which were set out in divisional booklets *Loadings of Passenger and Freight Trains*.

Sections from the Midland Division booklet setting out loadings for the Lickey Incline are shown in *Plate 136*, including the restrictions placed on 'down' trains, particularly mineral workings. Freight trains descending Lickey were required to stop at Blackwell and have brakes tied down, and to proceed slowly down the Bank, stopping at Bromsgrove (South) for brakes to be released.

L. M. S.—STEEPEST GRADIENTS.

	Section.	Gradient.	Distance
FOR GOODS AND PASSENGER TRAINS—			M. Chns.
Oldham Incline	L. & Y. ...	1 in 27½	64
Shawforth Branch	"	1 in 39	51
" "	"	1 in 41	42
" "	"	1 in 35	24
" "	"	1 in 34	47
Lickey Incline	Mid. ...	1 in 37½	2 5
Accrington Incline	L. & Y. ...	1 in 38	51
" "	"	1 in 40	1 7
Hemel Hempsted Branch ...	Mid. ...	1 in 38	25
Padiham Branch	L. & Y. ...	1 in 40	1 17
Atherton and Chequerbent ...	L. N. W. ...	1 in 30	72
" "	"	1 in 45	21
Leycett towards Halmerend ...	N. S. ...	1 in 31	32
Coniston Branch	Furness ...	1 in 49	27
Scotland—			
Leadhills Light Railway ...	Cal. ...	1 in 40	57
Girvan	G. & S. W. ...	1 in 55	3 60
Raven's Rock near Achterneed	Highland ...	1 in 50	1 75
" "	"	1 in 50	1 15
Colfin near Portpatrick	P. & W. Joint ...	1 in 56½	2 14
ON GOODS AND MINERAL LINE—			
*Middleton Incline	L. N. W. ...	1 in 8½	35
*Sheep Pasture Incline	"	1 in 8	25
(*On the Cromford & Parsley Hay Branch; worked by Stationary Engines.)	"	1 in 9	40
Hopton Incline	"	1 in 14	5
Scotland—			
Overtown Paper Mills Branch ...	Cal. ...	1 in 17	9
Bonnybridge Branch	"	1 in 19	54
" "	"	1 in 40	42
New Cumnock (Bank Line) ...	G. & S. W. ...	1 in 36	28

L. M. S.—HIGHEST ALTITUDES.

Summit or Station.	Section.	Feet above Sea level.
(a) Between Leadhills and Wanlockhead	Cal. ...	1,498
(b) Between Dalwhinnie and Dalnaspidal	Highland ...	1,484
(c) Wanlockhead Station	Cal. ...	1,412
Leadhills Station	"	1,405
Dalnaspidal Station	Highland ...	1,405
(d) Waenavon Station	L. N. W. ...	1,400
Between Carrbridge and Tomatin ...	Highland ...	1,315
Buxton District—		
Near Dowlow Lime Company's Works ...	L. N. W. ...	1,268
Between Nantybwch and Rhymney ...	L. N. W. & G. W. Jt. ...	1,216
Hindlow Station	L. N. W. ...	1,192
Between Hawes Junction and Kirkby Stephen	Mid. ...	1,167
Between Grantown-on-Spey and Dava ...	Highland ...	1,052
Between Elvanfoot and Beattock ...	Cal. ...	1,014
Between Ipstones and Winkhill ...	N. S. ...	999
Between Shawforth and Bacup ...	L. & Y. ...	965
Shap Summit	L. N. W. ...	915
Dove Holes Summit (Waterhouses Branch) ...	N. S. ...	900
Between Troutbeck and Penruddock ...	C. K. & P. ...	889
Between Muirkirk and Glenbuck ...	G. & S. W. ...	775
Between Forsinard and Altnabreac ...	Highland ...	708
Between Achnasheen and Achnashellach ...	"	646
Between Old Cumnock and New Cumnock ...	G. & S. W. ...	616
(a) Highest altitude in Great Britain		
(b) Highest altitude on any Main Line in Great Britain	On Standard Gauge Railways.	
(c) Highest station in Great Britain		
(d) Highest altitude and station in England or Wales ...		

Plate 136 (below & opposite): Loading of Passenger and Freight Trains for the Lickey Incline.

LOADING OF PASSENGER TRAINS, MAIN LINES (continued)

	LOAD IN TONS				
	CLASS OF PASSENGER ENGINE				
	2	3	4	5	5X
Bromsgrove to Blackwell:—					
Unassisted)	90	90	90	90	90
Assisted by one class 3 Freight Tank bank engine...	195	215	230	250	270
" " two " " " " " " "					
or one 2290 class bank engine.........................	295	315	330	350	370

When these loads are exceeded, three class 3 Freight Tank bank engines or one 2290 class bank engine and one Class 3 Freight Tank engine are necessary, except that double-headed trains may take up to 250 tons with one class 3 freight Tank bank engine

BETWEEN	NOTES	UP MINERAL Class of Engine								Maximum Number of wagons authorised	DOWN MINERAL Class of Engine								Maximum Number of wagons authorised
		1	2	3	4	5	6	7	8		1	2	3	4	5	6	7	8	
Bromsgrove to Blackwell...............	E	8	8	8	8	8	8	8	8	16	—	—	—	—	—	—	—	—	—
	F	20	22	24	26	27	29	30	33	60	—	—	—	—	—	—	—	—	—
	G	32	34	36	38	39	41	42	46	60	—	—	—	—	—	—	—	—	—
	H	44	46	48	48	51	53	54	59	60	—	—	—	—	—	—	—	—	—
Blackwell „ Bromsgrove		—	—	—	—	—	—	—	—	—	28	34	40	48	53	58	64	70	90

E—Unassisted.

F—Assisted by one Class 3 Freight Tank bank engine.

G— ,, ,, two ,, ,, ,, ,, ,, ,, or one 2290 class bank engine.

H— ,, ,, three ,, ,, ,, ,, ,, ,, ,, ,, ,, ,, ,, ,, and one Class 3 Freight Tank engine.

POINTS BETWEEN.	Notes.	CLASS OF TRAIN.					
		Fitted Freight No. 1.	Fitted Freight No. 2.	Express Freight ✠ (4 fully-fitted Vehicles connected up to the engine)	Express Freight.	Through Freight.	Mineral.
		Minutes	Minutes	Minutes	Minutes	Minutes	Minutes
UP TRAINS.		**GLOUCESTER TO BIRMINGHAM and Branches.**					
Bromsgrove to Blackwell	—	10	11	13	13	15	15
DOWN TRAINS.		**BIRMINGHAM TO GLOUCESTER and Branches.**					
Blackwell to Bromsgrove Sth.	—	7	7	10	12	13	15

Plate 137: Bromsgrove Station, looking north, up the Lickey Incline towards Blackwell, the rising gradient perceived beyond the bridge.

C. Gilbert

Plate 138: The gradient post beneath the bridge at the north end of Bromsgrove Station, and marking the commencement of the steepest main line gradient. The line to the south of the station was on a more leisurely grade.

J. Miller

Plate 139: Former Midland 2-4-0 No. 19 heads an LMS-built Compound 4-4-0 up the Lickey Incline, with the smoke plume from the banker visible above the train.

W. L. Good

Plate 140: The Lickey Banker falls away as the train on which the photographer was a passenger, gradually draws away. The massive cylinders and smokebox front show up well in this murky November 1937 view, as the train passes through Blackwell Station. The gradient at this point had eased to 1 in 291.

N. R. E. Williams

Plate 141: A pair of the Midland 0-6-0 3F tank engines, Nos 1947 and 1955, at Blackwell, standing on the 'up' main line.

W. L. Good

Plate 142: Another view of the banker, this time carrying the number plate 22290, and waiting to return down the bank to Bromsgrove.

W. L. Good

London Midland and Scottish
Railway Company
(G. & S. W. Section).

FROM

St. Enoch, GLASGOW

TO

CHELTENHAM

Plate 143: A mammoth support job, with the Lickey Banker and three 0-6-0 tank engines pushing a freight up the incline. The drivers are looking out of the cabs — even the guard is hanging his head out, not wishing to miss having his picture taken! One of the LMS official pictures for publicity purposes. *British Railways*

Plate 144: The desolate countryside in Westmorland through which the West Coast Main Line over Shap passed, is seen here as 3P 2-6-2T No. 16 banks a northbound freight up the four mile stretch of 1 in 75. This was the steepest gradient on the line between Euston and Carlisle. *E. E. Smith*

BRITISH EMPIRE EXHIBITION, WEMBLEY, 1925

The LMS attended this major exhibition and occupied several adjacent stands in the Palace of Engineering, where the major exhibits included the one 4-6-0 tender engine, No. 5845, built by Beardmore for the LMS to an earlier design supplied to the L&NWR. A third class vestibule carriage of the latest two-window design, one of a batch of fifty built at Derby, was also on exhibition, notable for the newly-introduced fawn and blue moquette upholstery, a departure from the standard black and red previously used.

No. 5845 was exhibited at Wembley before entering service, and for the duration of the exhibition was named *Prince of Wales*. In addition to several smaller features, a 60ft. length of fully-ballasted track using 95lb. per yard steel bullhead rail was exhibited with a sectioned piece of sleeper, chair and rail to give the public a closer look.

As with any exhibition, even in this day and age, the mountain of paperwork and literature available to the interested visitor was collosal, and the LMS was not slow in providing a wide assortment of brochures, timetables and other publicity material, both standard items and specially-produced issues. A forty page information booklet, with the front and rear covers featuring in full colour a picture of a third class vestibule coach was produced as a give-away entitled *Some Interesting Statistics of the LM&SR*. In it, figures ranging from the Company's capital figure, gross receipts split as to origin, mileage, numbers of passenger and goods stations, through to the steamer and hotel numbers, were carried, as well as rolling stock totals. Descriptions of the coach and engine exhibited, and photographs of the various stages of construction of rolling stock occupied more than half the pages — altogether an interesting momento of the Wembley Exhibition and the LMS stand in particular.

Plate 145: The cover and locomotive page from the Wembley booklet, the top edge of which was cut to the profile of the carriage roof, including ventilators.

Author's Collection

Plate 146: Two of the many notice boards made up to meet particular location requirements using a wooden base and individual cast letters.

J. Miller

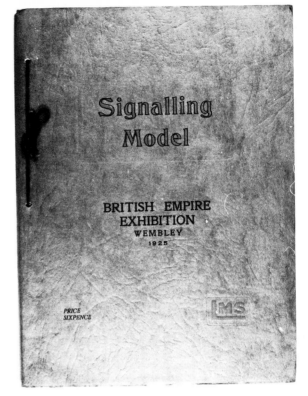

Plate 147: An LMS chair — note the wooden key is missing.

Author

Plate 148: Another feature at the Wembley Exhibition was a signalling model layout, and this booklet described its operation.

S. G. Underwood Collection

Plate 149: LMS steeplejacks at Inverness — an unlikely railway occupation!

Author's Collection

LMS EMPLOYEES IN A VARIETY OF OCCUPATIONS

In *LMS Miscellany (Volume II)*, an analysis of the various grades of employees is shown with the figures on the 31st December 1935 totalling 222,220. What these figures do not show is the variety of occupations that existed, and whilst it would be impossible to list every one, some interesting examples are shown in this section.

Plate 150 (bottom left): Telegraph linesmen aloft. Each white insulator, made out of pot, was stamped with the Company's initials — or the pre-group initials. The linesmen and the steeplejacks had the worst jobs of all in bad weather.

Author's Collection

Plate 151: Sand-blasting the paintwork off a tender down to the bare metal.

Author's Collection

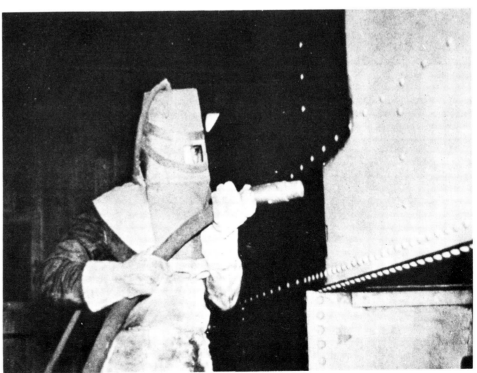

Plate 152: A 1937 Carriage Works picture, showing the automatic paint spraying machine which considerably reduced the time for carriage painting. The vehicle is one of the articulated corridor sets built at Derby in 1937, to Diagram 1965, brake third open and third open. A total of 22 pairs were built to Lot 1000.

British Railways

Plate 153: A paint shop craftsman applying the finishing touches.
Author's Collection

Plate 154: Provender millers at the Oakham Provender Depot — provender was feedstuff carefully prepared from a selection of ingredients and transported to all parts of the system to feed the Company's horse stock. Weekly output was 362 tons from Oakham, with similar provender mills located at Camden (London), Manchester and Glasgow. Total annual production of provender exceeded 36,000 tons.
Author's Collection

Plate 155: An LMS farrier at work, shoeing one of the Company's horses, a never-ending task. When the LMS came into being, on 1st January 1923, it inherited 9,079 road and 389 shunting horses. By the end of 1935 the total had dropped to 8,335, and by the end of 1946 it owned 6,168. The other three railway companies had slightly more than 10,000 between them at the Grouping, and only 3,000 in 1946. In the smaller stables, the local blacksmith was paid to attend to the horses, on average every three to four weeks, depending on the local roads and the nature of the work the horse undertook.

British Railways

Plate 156: A linesman walking his length of track near Barton and Walton Station, south of Burton on Trent. His job was to examine the length and to report any track defects, or if the wooden keys were working loose, to drive them home. Note the keys were driven into the chairs in the same directions as the trains travelled, and this point was highlighted in an Accident Prevention booklet for men working on or about the permanent way. Where there were several lines together, the permanent way men were warned to check the direction of a line by looking at the keys, although they were also warned this was not a foolproof check. The pathway was referred to as the cess, and the permanent way men were advised to keep to the cess as much as possible, facing the direction of approaching trains. It was a dangerous occupation if the utmost care was not exercised, and there were casualties as testimony to this.

V. R. Anderson Collection

LMS RESEARCH LABORATORY, DERBY

A detailed account of the research facilities available at Derby and the type of work undertaken is included in *LMS Miscellany (Volume I)* but photographs of these facilities were not available when that book was written. The accompanying photographs therefore show the laboratory which was opened on the 10th December 1935, by Lord Rutherford, OM, FRS, on London Road, Derby, adjacent to the Carriage & Wagon Works.

Plate 157: There were two connected blocks, the Laboratory Block on two floors, and an Engineering Test Room and Workshop Block, and provision was made for the addition of another floor to the Laboratory Block when this was required. The equipment throughout was of the latest design and technical specification.

B. Radford Collection

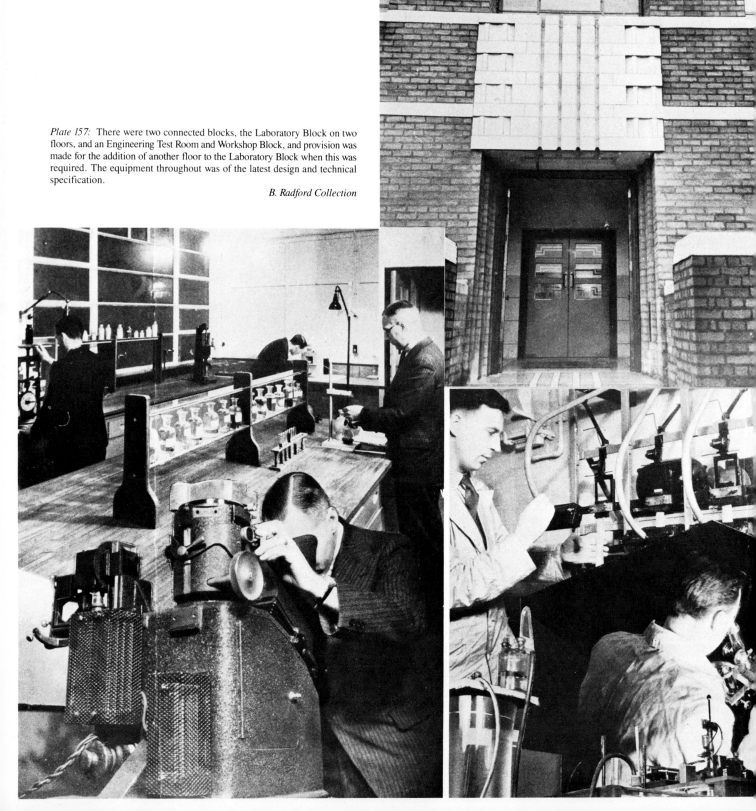

UNUSUAL MOTIVE POWER

In the two previous volumes, a number of unusual locomotives have been shown, and from comments and correspondence received, it has been suggested that some further photographs would be appreciated. The Ljungstrom turbine engine, and the high-pressure *Fury* are amongst the more unusual items featured in the next few views.

Plate 158: The former North Staffordshire Railway battery electric locomotive in LMS livery at Oakamoor, with what appears to be a very faint No. 2 on the middle plank above the nearest handail knob.

F. W. Shuttleworth

Plate 159: No. 6399 *Fury* in Derby Yard, a previously unpublished view of this interesting locomotive.

Author's Collection

Plates 160 & 161: Two official views of the Ljungstrom engine when new.

British Railways

Plate 162 (opposite upper): The same engine approaching St. Pancras Station in 1927 with a train from Derby, whilst undergoing trials.

British Railways

Plate 163 (opposite lower): This view of the engine attracting much attention at St. Pancras, with the condenser end of the unit up front for the return journey to Derby. The top of the condensing tank is shown to good effect, which should be of interest to any modellers wishing to reproduce this engine.

British Railways

Plate 164: The Ramsey-Armstrong Whitworth turbine electric condensing locomotive tried out on former L&YR metals, shown here at speed.

B. C. Lane Collection

AND PRE-GROUP COMPANY SIGNS REMAINED IN-SITU THROUGH THE LMS PERIOD

Plate 165: There were a wide variety of signs, cast iron and cast letters on a wooden base, which remained in use with a constant message, and these are but a few examples. Many remain, but as lines have closed, such signs have found an eager market with collectors.

J. Miller & G. Foxley Collections

LONDON & NORTH WESTERN RAILWAY

BEWARE OF THE **TRAINS**

LOOK BOTH UP & DOWN THE LINE BEFORE YOU CROSS

MIDLAND RAILWAY.

7 VICT. CAP. 18 SEC. 238 ENACTS "THAT IF ANY PERSON SHALL BE OR TRAVEL OR PASS UPON FOOT UPON THE MIDLAND RAILWAY WITHOUT THE LICENSE AND CONSENT OF THE MIDLAND RAILWAY COMPANY, EVERY PERSON SO OFFENDING SHALL FORFEIT AND PAY ANY SUM NOT EXCEEDING TEN POUNDS FOR EVERY SUCH OFFENCE." NOTICE IS THEREFORE HEREBY GIVEN THAT ALL PERSONS FOUND TRESPASSING UPON THIS RAILWAY OR THE WORKS THEREOF WILL BE PROSECUTED.

ALEXIS L. CHARLES.

JUNE 1899.

SECRETARY.

STRATFORD-UPON-AVON & MIDLAND JUNCTION RAILWAY.

BEWARE OF TRAINS.

TRESPASSERS WILL BE PROSECUTED

BY ORDER.

TRAVELLING POST OFFICE SERVICES ON THE LMS

The most famous TPO service on the LMS was the West Coast Postal, a title by which the 'down' special or 'up' special travelling post office trains were best known, travelling between Euston and Aberdeen, with sections to and from Edinburgh and Glasgow. The entire train consisted of specially-built carriages which allowed post office employees on the train to sort letters during the journey, and a number of baggage vans to carry parcels, and bags which had been sorted. TPO services ran overnight in most cases, and for much of the year the services were cloaked in darkness, and this has led to an inevitable shortage of photographs of such services.

The 'West Coast Postal' services connected at various points with other cross-country postal services, and before the timings of any service with a TPO carriage could be changed, the Post Office had to be approached and their agreement obtained. TPO services have been governed by Act of Parliament, and the Post Office pay for the cost of construction and maintenance of the special postal rolling stock, and this situation still applies to this day.

During World War II all postal sorting vehicles were withdrawn from service by September 1940, and were not returned to traffic until 1st October 1945, when sorting during the journey recommenced.

The exchange of bags of mail at speed with lineside apparatus was tried as early as 1837, and after several designs had been tested and problems with patents encountered, a John Dicker perfected the lineside apparatus design which continued in use from 1852 until lineside exchanges of mail ceased in October 1971. During the mid-1930 period, there were 33 apparatus points on the West Coast route, the first being only 8¼ miles out from Euston, at Wembley.

Tamworth was a key point of call for connections with the Midland TPO between Newcastle on Tyne and Bristol, and the Lincoln to Tamworth sorting carriage, but Crewe could boast eight intersecting postal services each night, one of which, the famous 'Irish Mail' following the same route from Euston, before taking the Chester and North Wales route out of Crewe.

The 'postal' train was turned at the end of each journey so that the apparatus could be used on the return journey. The other intresting feature about postal carriages was the side gangway connections, and they were, of course, unsuitable for corridor access to the normal coaching stock.

Plate 166: The 'up' 'Irish Mail' near Tamworth in August 1926, headed by ex-L&NWR 2-4-0 No. 1684 *Speke*, later renumbered 5029, and LMS Compound 4-4-0 No. 1150. The second carriage is a postal sorting vehicle. The side panels above the waist line are extended to take the letter sorting racks.

W. L. Good

Plate 167: The post office employee straps the mail pouch on to the arm, ready for collection, and beyond, the bag collection apparatus has been opened up ready for a drop.

Author's Collection

Plate 168: Lineside apparatus on the North Wales line. For use, the iron grid would be held vertical, and the horizontal bar holding it in place also detached the suspended bags from the train. The bag standard to the right was swung towards the track, and bags for collection were suspended from it.

Author's Collection

Plate 169: The 'down' special TPO – 'West Country Postal' – near Berkhamstead, with the extended net having just collected mail pouches from the lineside standard. The traductor brackets on the side of the train, for use when dropping mails, are clearly seen in the out-of-use position, and the side lights along the train are seen in this early evening picture. Note the wooden hut provided for the postal staff.

H. C. Casserley

Plates 170 & 171: Photographs to demonstrate the use of the extended traductor arms for dropping the mail pouches. Note the safety bars across the doorways. The lettering beneath the letter box instructs that an extra halfpenny fee must be affixed to letters posted on the train.

Plate 172: The traductor arm with mail pouch ready for dropping.
British Railways

Plate 173: An example of the wall-mounted posting box, a common feature at virtually every railway station. This one stood for many years at Brinklow Station.
G. Coltas

Plate 174: The interior of a sorting carriage, showing the bag racks on the left and the letter racks on the right. Strong leather padding was fitted to all parts of the structure which protruded, to provide some protection for those working in the vehicle when it was at speed.
The Post Office, Crown Copyright

Plate 175: The 'down' special TPO at Crewe during the 13 minute stop. Here an interchange of mail bags with seven other TPO services takes place, and the Manchester and Liverpool stowage vans are taken off the main train, whilst vans from Birmingham for Glasgow and Edinburgh are added to it. This view, in 1934, close to midnight, shows the activity which ensures all bags are correctly routed. The trolleys are not railway owned, but provided by the Post Office.

The Post Office, Crown Copyright

Plate 176: An LMS Northern Counties Committee sorting carriage being loaded in Belfast Station in 1935.

The Post Office, Crown Copyright

INTERNAL LETTER SORTING ARRANGEMENTS

From 1st August 1928, the LMS introduced a standard system for its own correspondence, and 79 letter sorting stations were set up around the system. Every station was grouped to one of these sorting centres and Company correspondence was addressed with the appropriate code — a letter addressed to the goods agent at Coventry, would have 'LMS5' added. Sorting station No. 5 was at Rugby, and that centre was responsible for passing the incoming correspondence to the appropriate station within its area by the next available service. Some stations were allocated two or more sorting centre numbers — mail for Ashby-de-la-Zouch could be routed through three centres; No. 8 (Nuneaton), No. 50 (Burton on Trent) or No. 57 (Leicester), the centre used which was best served by the train service from the forwarding point.

To minimise the sorting, only one envelope per day could be used for all correspondence from one station or office to another, and envelopes travelled with the guard on each train. Correspondence between offices and/or stations where there was a direct service from the forwarding point was not to be routed through this system, and any registered items, items of value and newsletters were excluded from the letter sorting arrangements. Envelopes addressed to collieries and sidings had to have the name of the nearest station and the code for that station. More than forty years elapsed before a countrywide system of postal codes was originated by the Post Office — the LMS letter codes were system-wide.

Plate 177: A sticky label for affixing to envelopes and below it the address panel which was printed on the reverse of letter forms, ready for completion by the originating officer.

Author's Collection

FROM CENTRE No.................Date......./......./19....

LETTER SORTING CENTRE,
L. M. & S. R.
ACCRINGTON
Centre No. **34.**

Plate 178: The LMS encouraged employees to participate in a variety of activities, with first aid and ambulance work a widespread and widely followed interest, with participants no strangers to success, and the trophies which came with it, as this photograph of the Ashbourne team shows.

(The original print is in poor condition).

Dr. J. Hollick Collections

Chief Parcel Clerk,

London Midland and Scottish Railway Company,

Church Station

(L M S. 34)

ASHBOURNE L.M. & S. AMBULANCE TEAM who have won the Holmes Challenge Trophy (N.S. Area). Mr. Thornhill (Stationmaster), H. Green (Captain), N. Shephard, J. Hughes, H. Gallimore and W. Hand.

DIESEL LOCOMOTIVES USED BY THE LMS

In the two previous *LMS Miscellany* volumes, illustrations of diesel passenger trains and railcars used by the Company have been featured, including those which underwent trials, but were never owned by the Company. With each type they were a form of experimentation, but diesel shunting locomotives became a more permanent inclusion in the Company's motive power lists, and they were used over a wide area.

In 1931, a withdrawn 0-6-0 tank locomotive No. 1831 was stripped down to its frames and wheels and converted to become the first diesel-hydraulic shunter for the Company. The frames and wheels were fitted with a 400hp Davey Paxman 6 cylinder oil engine with hydraulic transmission supplied by Haslam & Newton, and it left Derby Works for trials in 1932, eventually being taken back into LMS stock in 1934.

At this time a number of private manufacturers were building diesel locomotives, and the Company contracted to purchase from several of them. The first came from Hunslet, a diesel mechanical 0-6-0 shunter No. 7401, followed by others from the same manufacturer, but each with a different type of engine. Hudswell Clarke, the Drewry Car Co., and Harland & Wolfe, were other manufacturers who supplied the LMS, and by the end of 1935 there were nine diesel shunters at work and undergoing evaluation. Although they were referred to as diesel locomotives, there was some argument as to whether they should be more correctly described as high-speed heavy-oil engines. The term 'diesel' came from Rudolph Diesel's Patent of 1892, which covered slow-speed compression ignition engines, and through progressive development of this type of propulsion, the term 'diesel' was extended to describe the high-speed engine also.

In 1936 Armstrong Whitworth and Hawthorn Leslie provided a further twenty one shunters and, together with the earlier machines, constituted the diesel shunter fleet until 1939, when ten were built at Derby Works, followed by further batch production in the early war years. A number of diesel shunters were loaned or sold to the War Department for war service, and some went overseas.

With the early diesel mechanical shunters, there were some transmission problems and they were not entirely suited for the heavy duty work, whereas the diesel electric engines soon proved their superiority and reliability for all duties.

Batch production of shunters continued at Derby after the war, and the development of diesel traction for express work was taken forward by the LMS in 1947, with the delivery of a Co-Co diesel electric. No. 10000, in December 1947, less than a month before the absorption of the Company into British Railways. It was built at Derby with English Electric 1,600hp traction motors, and intended for suburban and semi-fast passenger trains when operating as a single unit, or for use on express work when in tandem with a sister unit, No. 10001, which in the event did not enter service until 1948.

The accompanying photographs show examples of the diesel fleet used by the Company.

Plate 179: Five shunters under construction in the Hawthorne Leslie works, to an English Electric design, in 1935.

T. Collinge Collection

1—2/32.   E.R.O. 21556/50

L. M. S. R.

DUNFERMLINE

Plate 180: The engine being lowered into the frames. The cabside plate reads English Electric 1935 Hawthorne Leslie.

T. Collinge Collection

Plate 181: The second of a batch of five, built in 1935, which entered service in 1936, No. 7070, one of those transferred for War Department service at the outbreak of war, and lost in 1940.

T. Collinge Collection

Plate 182: The first of the 0-6-0 diesel mechanical shunters built by The Hunslet Engine Company, No. 7051, originally allocated the number 7401. It is seen in Crewe South Shed Yard on 15th August 1937 with black-shaded initials. No. 7161 was one of the four Sentinel 2-cylinder chain-driven steam locomotives built in 1930. An Armstrong Whitworth 0-6-0 shunter, No. 7063, is seen in the background.

N. R. E. Williams

Plate 183: A small 0-4-0 diesel mechanical shunter built by The English Electric Company at Preston, with bodywork provided by The Drewry Car Company of Burton on Trent. When ordered, it was allocated the number 7400, but it entered LMS service renumbered as No. 7050.

T. Collinge Collection

Plate 184 (left): A line-up of diesel shunters, seven built by Hawthorn Leslie, with the sole Sentinel Doble Compound No. 7192 the odd man out.

Author's Collection

Plate 186 (opposite upper): No. 10000, the first main line diesel express locomotive, and the forerunner of express diesel locomotive types on British Railways. Delivered in December 1947, and immediately placed on test between Derby and St. Pancras, it is seen at Millersdale Station en route to Manchester with the dynamometer car behind the locomotive. It was soon followed by a sister engine, No. 10001, but by this time the LMS, as a separate railway company, had ceased, and British Railways had been formed. Tests were also carried out on the West Coast Main Line from Euston, and the two locomotives were paired and used on the 'Royal Scot' service to Glasgow.

M. L. Knighton Collection

Plate 187 (opposite lower): On the 18th December 1947, the press were invited to join a special train from Euston to Watford, and return with No. 10000 at the head of the special, and here the locomotive is seen at Euston alongside Stanier Pacific No. 6256 *Sir William A. Stanier F.R.S.*, which was also a new engine, having been turned out of Crewe five days prior to this picture being taken.

British Railways

Plate 185: A Derby-built shunter of 1939, with jackshaft drive requiring a longer wheelbase and frame arrangement. No. 7087 is pictured at Willesden in June 1946.

V. Forster Collection

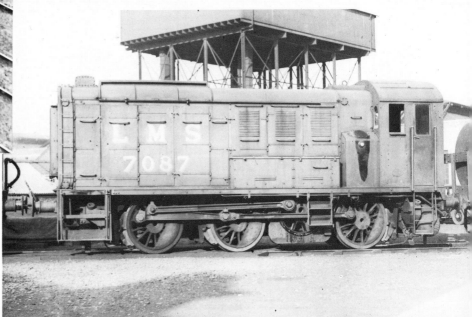

GENERAL TRAFFIC

The following plates are a miscellaneous selection of general traffic scenes around the system, typical of the everyday workings of a railway.

Plate 188: An express freight, a fitted van train travelling north on the long straight stretch to Tamworth behind an unidentified 2-6-0 'Crab', as these engines were nicknamed. The first van is white with black lettering.

Railways Yesteryear Collection

Plate 189: Fourteen vans making up a pigeon special, photographed near Willesden. The white headboard is in fact a lettered piece of paper placed upon the original photograph and rephotographed for publicity purposes to attract pigeon traffic.

National Railway Museum

Plate 190: An ex-L&NWR 0-6-0 heading a freight train through the wide area of trackwork alongside Carlisle (Upperby) Shed, in June 1936.

V. Forster Collection

Plate 191: A 7F 0-8-0, No. 9673, one of the last batch constructed in 1932 and fitted with ACFI feed water heaters, at the head of a heavy freight train, with what appears to be military equipment sheeted down. Immediately behind the tender and guard's van is the largest vehicle built by the LMS, the sole 120 ton bogie trolley. No. 300000.

G. Coltas

Plate 192: East Croydon Station on the Southern Railway, with LMS 0-6-2 tank No. 7755 on a transfer freight, with the CWS road tanker aboard a 6-wheel wagon, behind the bunker.

V. Forster Collection

LMS **TO PAY** E.R.O. 51728

PARCEL LABEL

From_____

To_____

		s.	d.
	Paid on ...		
No. of Packages	Collection ...		
	Carriage C.R.		
	,, O.R.		
	To Collect ...		

Plate 193: A train-load of welded mild steel containers on LMS long low wagons awaiting movement in Wicker Goods Yard, Sheffield.

Davy McKee Ltd.

Plate 194: A huge load, en-route from Sheffield to Stalingrad in the Soviet Union, loaded on the former Midland 60 ton trolley, No. 5100.
Davy McKee Ltd.

Plate 195: A 25 ton load in the Wicker Goods Yard, Sheffield. The two intensifier stools are for a forging press, and are typical of the larger castings carried by rail.

Davy McKee Ltd.

Plate 196: The first 7F 0-8-0 locomotive, No. 9500, built in 1929 at Crewe, trundles a train of vans along the slow line. The varying roof heights show well in this view on the North-West main line.

Railways Yesteryear Collection

LONDON MIDLAND AND
SCOTTISH RAILWAY COMPANY.

P. F. 70.
R 2a

SHEFFIELD

Plate 197: A former L&NWR 0-4-2 crane tank, No. 3246, in Crewe Station, being used to manoeuvre a heavy casting.
V. Forster Collection

R O. 21514

L M S

Description of }
Consignment } ....

From ....

To ....

Date ....

Train ....

LIVE STOCK
HANDLE WITH CARE.

(This label to be used to denote that a "Higher Value" charge has been paid on this Consignment.)

Plate 198: Freight on the Highland Section, north of Inverness. 'Jones' Highland 4-6-0 class locomotive No. 17919, heads a long mixed freight through Muir of Ord. The Black Isle line referred to on the nameboard refers to the line to Fortrose. This design was the first British 4-6-0 tender engine design when introduced in 1894. Note the lettering on the seat back and rail.

Lens of Sutton

Plate 199: No. 5827, an un-named 'Prince of Wales' class 4-6-0, heads an 'up' express just south of Tamworth (Low Level) Station, seen in the left background.

Railways Yesteryear Collection

Plate 200: A Stanier 2-6-2T arrives at Motherwell on 2nd August 1938 with a local passenger train, with the tall Caledonian lattice signal indicating a clear road.

L. Hanson

Plate 201: Former Caledonian 4-6-0 No. 14768 *Clan Mackenzie* leaves Glasgow (Buchanan Street) on 21st June 1938. Note the painted letters on the gable end of the building, a feature common on buildings adjacent to the railway.

H. C. Casserley

Plate 202: Former Highland 4-6-0 No. 14688 *Thurso Castle* heads a passenger working near Killiercrankie in 1926.

P. Tatlow Collection

THE EXECUTIVE RESEARCH OFFICE

Plates 203 & 204:

These two photographs show sections of the ERO section — The Executive Research Office — which was established to carry out a complete overhaul of the Company's arrangements for all printed matter, including advertising, operating publications, including timetables, and the vast plethora of departmental forms. As recorded in *LMS Miscellany (Volume I) — Plate 244,* Canadian consultants were employed in 1928 to review the multiplicity of printed material in use, and eliminate waste, and considerable savings were achieved from this exercise. The consultants were paid on the amount saved.

Arising out of the investigations, many changes were introduced, and a centralised control procedure was set up to deal with the design, purchase, storage and distribution, and the standardisation of the qualities, weights and sizes of paper to ensure these all met the varied requirements for running a railway.

The Executive Research Office was responsible for the planned purchase of paper in bulk to meet expected requirements, and they supplied the various printers used by the Company with the paper in the sizes required for production to LMS specifications.

The office also received copies of circulars, returns and statistics, requirements which the various departments were proposing to issue, using any of the mechanical duplicating processes, and which were not of any urgent nature. The ERO would determine the best method to adopt for production. For urgent material the department concerned would produce the particular circular or return and forward a copy to the ERO for their assessment and advice as to the production of any similar material in the future.

In all cases, where printing was required, the material had to be sent to the ERO for consideration, and the department concerned would now be required to respond to a variety of searching questions as to the need for any new form, or return, or statistical information, prior to approval being given and production started.

Through this centralised control procedure, the Executive Research Office was in a position to use the latest techniques in the printing industry as appropriate, and one of the principal changes in production was applied to producing the Company's public timetables, using the photo offset process, with its progressive use applied to other requirements. This process saved the Company considerable expenditure, by eliminating thousands of hours of compilation and typesetting.

The standardised paperwork carried an ERO reference number, and in some instances the pre-group company reference also for ease of identification in the early period after the formation of the ERO.

British Railways

Plate 205: The Company provided pencils — 90269 was the reference for those supplied to the clerical passenger and office staff; 90256 had a thick lead, and was supplied to goods yard and warehouse staff for marking cartons or wagon labels with easily legible writing.

G. Waite Collection

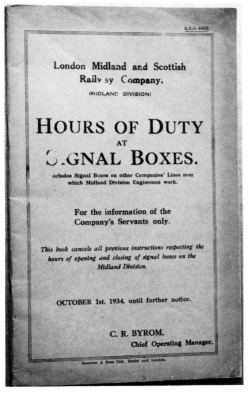

London Midland and Scottish
Railway Company.

(MIDLAND DIVISION)

HOURS OF DUTY
AT
SIGNAL BOXES.

Includes Signal Boxes on other Companies' Lines over
which Midland Division Enginemen work.

**For the information of the
Company's Servants only.**

*This book cancels all previous instructions respecting the
hours of opening and closing of signal boxes on the
Midland Division.*

OCTOBER 1st. 1934, until further notice.

C. R. BYROM,
Chief Operating Manager.

E.R.O. 46187

Admit Miss *Miller*
to the Hunt's Bank Approach at Manchester
(Victoria) Station to witness the arrival of
Their Majesties the King and Queen on Tuesday,
17th July, 1934.

BY ORDER.

July, 1934.

Plate 206: Various items with ERO
reference, and there are many others
elsewhere in this volume.
46423 — G. Foxley Collection
46187 — J. Miller Collection

LMS   E.R.O. 59029
Via BATH and
L. M. & S. Rly.

BARROWS & TROLLEYS

In *LMS Miscellany (Volume I)* the section of notes and nine plates *(Plates 71-79)* showing the construction and types of barrows and trolleys was of particular interest to modellers, and as there were so many types in use throughout the LMS period, a further selection will no doubt be of interest to the modelling fraternity. Those built by the Company were stamped on the woodwork, and most wheels had the LMS letters cast in. Details of the allocations of barrows and trolleys are given in *Volume I*, but many of the older pre-group types were retained at some locations in addition to the LMS standard types.

Plate 207: This type 210 was the Midland heavy 2-wheel platform barrow, and its Midland origins are evidenced by the impressed MR9115 above the wheel. This was the third version, the earlier ones having outside wheels initially, and the second version having different bar spacing on the end ironwork. A later version had the horizontal bars rivetted to the end ironwork. Many of these heavy barrows have continued in use to the present day.

Author's Collection

Plate 209: An oddity! The trolley is basically a type 200 wooden 9ft. one, but with a specially constructed body which was referred to officially as an 'Ice Cream Shute'. It was used for off-loading heavy containers from vans and wagons, by using this to slide them on to another trolley parked alongside. This was not a sole example as there were others on a 6ft. type 201 framework, some left-hand and some right-hand. This example was photographed in January 1939. The clip to retain the handle was not fitted to the normal type 200 and 201s.

Author's Collection

Plate 210: The steel welded type 200 trolley introduced in the early 1930s. It was 9ft. in length, but 3ft. 6in. wide, some 3in. narrower than the wooden type 200, and with a platform height almost 4in. lower than the wooden trolley. The paint date is 28th July 1939.

Author's Collection

Plate 208 (opposite lower): Barrow Station, on 11th February 1930, with a pair of Furness Railway handcarts on the pavement, and in the foreground, a heavy duty sling trolley, probably photographed so that similar examples could be constructed.

Author's Collection

Plate 211: A provender barrow for use in stables. Provender was the foodstuff for the Company's horses, although this example has been relegated to carrying wood chippings only. The paint date is 23rd February 1939.

Author's Collection

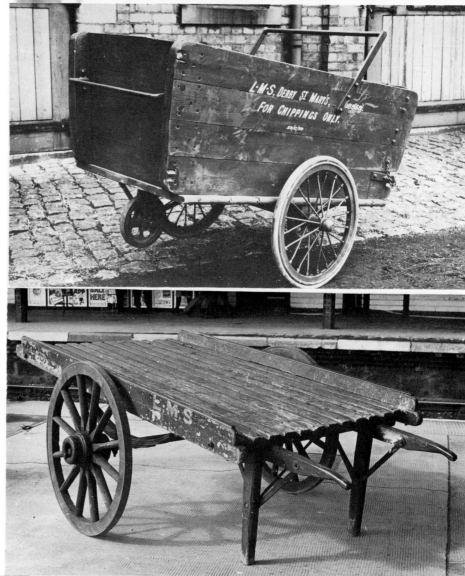

Plate 212 (right): A 2-wheel handcart of Highland Railway origin, known as the 'Hurley', seen here at Aviemore. This, and other similar 2-wheel handcarts, were more commonly used on the Highland Section of the Northern Division than the 4-wheel trolley types.

Author's Collection

Plate 213: The 1 ton Harbuilt battery-operated trolley purchased in quantity by the LMS from the manufacturer. The handle movement downwards activated the trolley, and it was capable of towing loaded flat trolleys.

Author's Collection

Plate 214: This truck was designated an earthenware crate truck Standard type 262, and as the station name signifies, allocated for use in the Potteries area. Note the forked-end ironwork, and LMS is just visible on the hub caps.

Author's Collection

Plate 215: The type 261 deck trolley introduced in early 1939 for use in warehouses and goods sheds. The mechanical brake apparatus was a new addition to this type of trolley, and with a swing of the lever, the two front caster wheels were raised clear of the ground.

Author's Collection

A MISCELLANY WITHIN A MISCELLANY!

A further selection of 'items LMS' which were to be seen in varying quantities around the system, taken for granted then, but now collectors' items to many.

Plate 216: This spoon is lettered 'LMS Rifle Clubs' — by 1938 there were eleven clubs for LMS staff in various centres, organised into a federation system to promote competitions between the centres, and with outside clubs. A winter league was the principal Company competition, with teams divided into two divisions in accordance with their levels of proficiency. An annual rifle meeting competition was held at Derby and open to all LMS riflemen, whether members of a club or not, and prizes were awarded. Inter-railway matches were at the famous Bisley range, whilst international matches were held at a London range or the Derby range. One major benefit for the individual members was that they were able to purchase ammunition and equipment at cheaper prices as a result of the federation's bulk purchasing power.

A small number of the clubs used .303 bore military weapons, whilst most used the small bore .22 'miniature' rifle. The advantage with the small bore weapon was that it was relatively cheap, competitions could be carried on in any weather outdoors, and was ideal for the smaller indoor ranges. LMS staff entered the national competitions and were occasionally amongst the trophy winners. Spoons of the type shown here were won in the LMS in-house competitions.

J. Kay Collection

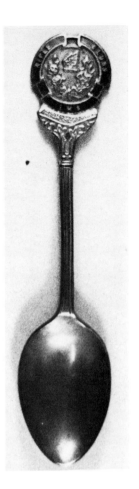

Plate 217: Signal and point fittings were also cast with the Company initials, and this type of wire pulley came in single, twin, three or four wire sizes. They were placed at intervals, 20ft. to 30ft. apart, or where the wire needed to change direction.

G. Foxley Collection

Plate 218: A dual-purpose wooden cradle — for use either as a saw bench or stand for a creosote or paraffin drum.

J. Miller

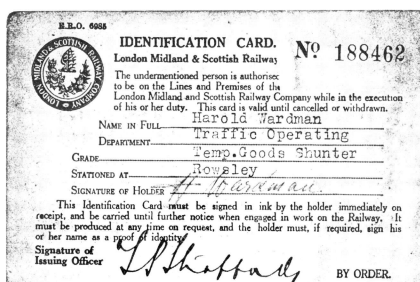

LMS
No. `1424`

The Bearer of this Card is employed in a grade entitling him when on Duty to purchase refreshment at any canteen provided on Railway Premises for the use of H.M. Forces by the organisations comprising the Council of Voluntary War Work or other approved body at times and places where refreshment facilities provided by the Railways for their own Staff do not exist.

Permission given for the purpose of Refreshments does not entitle the holder of the permit to purchase Cigarettes, Chocolate, Sweets or Cosmetics.

Name in full ___ WARDMAN. H.
Grade ___ Goods Guard.
Stationed at ___ ROWSLEY. 49.
Signature of Holder ___
Signature of Issuing Officer ___
Designation ___
Date 1 0 SEP 1946

E.R.O. 52207.

E.R.O. 6985
IDENTIFICATION CARD.
London Midland & Scottish Railway
Nº 188462

The undermentioned person is authorised to be on the Lines and Premises of the London Midland and Scottish Railway Company while in the execution of his or her duty. This card is valid until cancelled or withdrawn.

NAME IN FULL ___ Harold Wardman
DEPARTMENT ___ Traffic Operating
GRADE ___ Temp.Goods Shunter
STATIONED AT ___ Rowsley
SIGNATURE OF HOLDER ___ H Wardman

This Identification Card must be signed in ink by the holder immediately on receipt, and be carried until further notice when engaged in work on the Railway. It must be produced at any time on request, and the holder must, if required, sign his or her name as a proof of identity.

Signature of
Issuing Officer ___   BY ORDER.

Plate 219: Two card passes, typical of the many types issued to employees. No. 1424 is particularly interesting. It does not permit the holder to purchase items which were on ration book issue in any case.

H. Wardman Collection

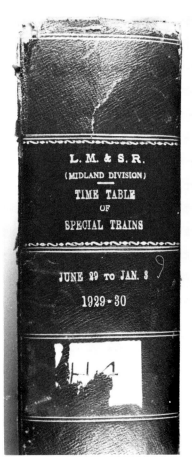

L.M. & S.R.
(MIDLAND DIVISION)
TIME TABLE
OF
SPECIAL TRAINS

JUNE 29 to JAN. 3
1929-30

Plate 221: And to take the biscuit . . . an LMS biscuit tin used by the Hotel Services.

J. Miller Collection

Plate 220: Working timetables for passenger and freight workings covered the regular scheduled services, but, in addition to these, weekly divisional 'Programmes of Special Trains' were issued approximately five days before the seven day period they covered. Any late additions or cancellations were promulgated in a special 'Supplementary Programme of Special Trains' notice distributed throughout the appropriate division. The official binder shown here is 3in. thick and covers a six month period.

G. Waite Collection

INSURANCE

The Railway Passengers Assurance Company advertised throughout the railway network, using enamelled signs, posters and handbills, and the railway companies themselves issued tickets giving insurance cover through all station booking and enquiry offices. The premium rates charged appear modest.

BR. 63

TRAVEL CARE FREE

SEND YOUR LUGGAGE IN ADVANCE

ASK FOR DETAILS AT YOUR LOCAL STATION

Plate 222: Both sides of the handbill issued in January 1938.

Author's Collection

INSURANCE TICKETS

for

YOURSELF

and for

YOUR LUGGAGE

can be obtained at all

L M S

BOOKING OFFICES

•

Railway Passengers Assurance Company

WISE *or* OTHERWISE?

What about your Baggage when you go away — ?

Be wise and Insure it with the

RAILWAY PASSENGERS ASSURANCE CO.

AGAINST ALL LOSS ANYWHERE

AGENT AT THIS OFFICE

You insure your Valuables and Effects at Home
Do you protect them in your Baggage when Travelling ?

The Insurance is cheap, convenient and comprehensive. It applies during transit of the baggage by Land, Sea or Air or while the owner is staying at Hotels or elsewhere. It provides for loss (Fire and Theft included) of the insured articles ; it covers damage due to Fire, Sea-water, Derailment, Collision of train or boat, or arising from a vessel being stranded or sunk.

N.B.—The Company's liability in respect of Damage is strictly limited, as above.

AVAILABLE IN ALL PLACES AND SITUATIONS IN AND BETWEEN GREAT BRITAIN, IRELAND, ISLE OF MAN, ISLE OF WIGHT AND CHANNEL ISLANDS.

AMOUNT INSURED	PREMIUM.		
	Fifteen Days.	Three Weeks.	One Calendar Month.
£20	1/-	1/6	2/-
£40	2/-	3/-	4/-
£60	3/-	4/6	5/-
£100	5/-	6/-	7/6

N.B.—The Company will not be liable in respect of any loss or damage when the amount thereof does not exceed 10/.

ANYWHERE IN THE WORLD. (Requisite proposal to be obtained of Booking Agent.)

AMOUNT INSURED	PREMIUM.				
	Fifteen Days.	Three Weeks.	One Month.	Two Months.	For periods longer than 2 months or for amounts of more than £500, rates will be furnished on application
£25	2/-	3/-	4/-	5/-	
£50	4/-	6/-	8/-	10/-	
£75	6/-	9/-	12/-	15/-	
£100	8/-	12/-	16/-	20/-	

Available for Baggage accompanied by a Passenger, also for carted Luggage and Luggage sent in advance.

Subject to conditions printed on the Tickets.

RAILWAY PASSENGERS ASSURANCE CO.

Head Office :
64 Cornhill, London, E.C. 3.

R.P. 228 (R
W.B. 7-38 30m

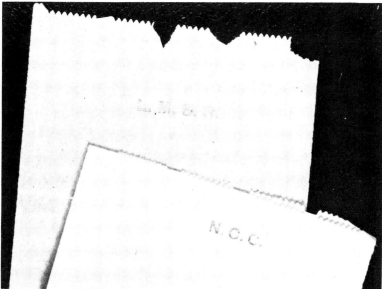

Plate 223: Toilet roll holders in carriages and waiting rooms were cast in brass with prominent letters.

G. Foxley Collection

Plate 224: And guess what . . . even the toilet tissue was stamped in black!

D. Tee Collection

Plate 225: A piece of blacked board to take chalked messages, which was of a size which allowed for it to be displayed in a booking office window, or an outward-facing one.

G. Foxley Collection

Plate 226: A small plastic envelope given out by the LMS Northern Friendly Society, still with offices in Glasgow today. The plastic folder is a recent issue.

D. P. Rowland

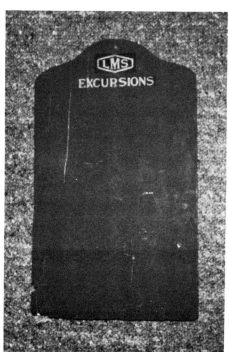

L. M. S. R.

E.R.O. 21556/95
2/33

LONGPORT

Plate 227: This 12-page pamphlet was for the staff in the difficult days after the war when the railways were trying to recreate the image of service to the public. The Chief Commercial Manager's message commenced — inter alia — 'It is very important that there should be no slackening of effort to maintain and indeed improve the efficiency of the railway service. We need to demonstrate collectively that the LMS is in all respects a well-run undertaking in which the staff have a pride. Our job is to provide and sell transport. To discharge this responsibility successfully we must provide facilities which will attract the customer. The provision and development of these is the responsibility of the management. The exploitation of them is the responsibility of the staff.' So much of what is written in this staff pamphlet remains true and valid in today's world: 'Always be courteous and helpful. If the caller is irate or even rude, there is no need for you also to lose your temper. Don't forget to end a conversation with a polite 'Thank you'.

Author's Collection

Plate 228: The LMS internal telephone system linked all parts of the system, in addition to the public telephone connections, and this directory was issued to all departments in the area shown on the cover.

J. Kay Collection

Plate 229: A selection of the glossy brochures issued for tourists in the 1920s and 1930s. The LMS and LNER combined to issue a series; *The Land of Scott & Burns* and *Through the Trossachs* were but two of the titles, both with maps of their respective areas. The LMS Series *Scotland for Holidays* were issued for a number of areas: '*Oban and the Land of Lorne; Strathspey and the Moray Firth; The Central Highlands* were part of this series.

Author's Collection

Plate 230: A booklet setting out the cheap fares available and the terms on which they were issued. Winter Resort Tickets, Anglers' tickets, and Friends of Ocean Passengers tickets were amongst those described, the latter class of traffic being restricted to the ocean-going ports of Glasgow, Greenock, Birkenhead, Liverpool, Manchester, Southampton, Plymouth, Avonmouth Docks, Cardiff (General), Swansea, Portland, Weymouth and Hull. Ocean shipping companies issued vouchers to the relatives and friends of those booked for sea travel, and these were exchanged for tickets to the port of departure which were valid for a five-day period including day of issue.
Burton to Wick £11 5s 3d, Burton to Penzance £6 4s 3d, or Burton to Horninglow, 2d!
G. Waite Collection

Plate 231: The pre-war set of LMS postcards which were issued in an enveloped set as well as singly. The post-war was shown in *LMS Miscellany (Volume II) — Plate 139.*
Author's Collection

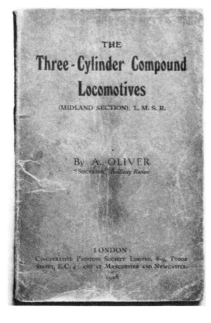

SINGLE LINE WORKING — TABLET EXCHANGE

Safety for trains on single line sections is of paramount importance. Tablets were kept in instruments at signal cabins at either end of a single line section, and as a train entered a section, the fireman took a tablet, surrendering it at the opposite end of the section. A leather pouch was used for convenience when exchanging the tablet for the particular stretch of line.

In these scenes the exchange of tablets is seen taking place at Crossmichael Station on the line between Dumfries and Stranraer, on the former Portpatrick & Wigtownshire Joint Line (Jt. Cal., G&SW, L&NW, & Mid). The maximum speed permitted was 10m.p.h. to prevent the fireman or signalman from receiving arm and shoulder injuries which could result if the speed was higher. As an experiment, leather arm sleeves were issued, but these proved to be time-consuming to fit and cumbersome, and they were discarded, with the maximum speed limit being enforced. There were three main types of automatic exchange apparatus used on LMS lines, Bryson's, Whitaker's and Manson's, and for the last two of these to be used, the locomotives using the line had to be fitted with cabside catching gear. The fireman could use a hand-held device with Bryson's apparatus. When locomotives without the gear fitted used the line, hand-exchange was resorted to.

Plate 232: Crossmichael Station was situated between two single line sections, and here the fireman prepares to surrender the tablet for the section through which he has run, and to collect that for the section he is proceeding into.

British Railways

Plate 233 (opposite upper): The moment of exchange — note with the train engine, not the pilot, as the driver of the train engine was responsible for the safety of the train. The clip above the engine number was for fitting Bryson's catching gear to the cabside.

British Railways

Plate 234 (opposite lower): Automatic tablet exchange taking place using Bryson's apparatus alongside the Crossmichael signal cabin in 1946. The cabside gear is just discernible.

British Railways

DOUBLE-HEADED TRAINS

These were always of interest to the lineside observer, to say nothing of those whose main interest lay in number-taking sessions at the stations. Some of the heavy trains were rostered for two engines to ensure booked times were maintained throughout the journey, and as the Midland Section's largest passenger engine was the Compound 4-4-0, a second engine was commonplace on the Midland Division until the 'Royal Scots', and later the 'Jubilees' were introduced. There was always the possibility of a second engine being placed at the head of a train, even the less heavily-loaded workings, if there was no booked return duty for the engine concerned to work back to its 'home' shed, or it was needed to 'place' the engine ready to work a turn from another point on the system. Where this requirement was not done by double-heading, a light engine working would be made. The following section provides an interesting selection of such workings.

Plate 235: Un-named 'Patriot' 4-6-0 No. 5522 heads a Class 5 4-6-0 locomotive on an empty stock working at Kensington (Addison Road).
V. Forster Collection

Plate 236: Two unidentified former London & North Western engines — a 'Precursor' and 'Claughton', head north with a 15-coach express a mile north of Lichfield (Trent Valley) Station in the 1930s.
Author's Collection

Plate 237: Tender to tender, two former Midland 0-6-0s, 2F No. 2976 and 3F No. 3342, head a long line of coal wagons near Loughborough in May 1927. Soon afterwards the Beyer-Garratt engines were introduced to the heaviest workings on the Midland main line.

W. L. Good

Plate 238: A pair of 4F 0-6-0s on a football excursion between Derby and Burton on Trent, Nos. 4291 and 4067. This was a regular combination of motive power for excursion workings, particularly at weekends when the 4Fs were not on normal freight duty.

W. L. Good

Plate 239: On another part of the Midland main line out of St. Pancras, former LT&SR 4-6-4T No. 2106 leads ex-Midland 2P 4-4-0 No. 555 on a 6-coach working at Mill Hill in 1923.

The late A. G. Ellis

Plate 240: A pair of Scottish constituent engines leaving Aviemore on 18th June 1927 with a train of mixed origin carriages. Ex-Glasgow & South Western 4-4-0 No. 14375 leads a former Highland 4-6-0 'Clan' class engine, No. 14766 *Clan Chattan*.

H. C. Casserley

Plate 241: A Barrow-in-Furness departure, with ex-L&NWR No. 5104 *Woodlark* and former Furness 4-6-4T No. 11102 ready for the green light in 1931. The ex-L&NWR 2-4-0s were regularly used as pilot engines in the early LMS period.

G. Coltas

Plate 242: A 3F, No. 3308, coasts through the Peak District with a new Beyer-Garratt, No. 4997, and a brake van.
Railways Yesteryear Collection

Plate 243: An ex-works trio passes the water softening plant on a trial run — 'Claughton' No. 5925 *E. C. Trench*, 'Precursor' class No. 5282 *Champion* and 'Royal Scot' No. 6143 *Mail*. The nameplate on No. 6143 appears to be single line with a brass plate beneath which would have depicted an engraving of the earlier locomotive carrying this name. No. 6143 was later re-named *The South Staffordshire Regiment* in 1934.

W. L. Good

Plate 244: Two former Midland engines: 3F 0-6-0 No. 3606 leading a 4F 0-6-0 on a mixed freight train.
Railways Yesteryear Collection

Plate 245: Liverpool (Lime Street) and Lowestoft (Central) were linked by a through service, with a journey time in excess of 7 hours. The Liverpool portion left Lime Street at 10.25a.m., Crewe at 11.20a.m. and was joined with the Manchester and Stockport through carriages at Stoke-on-Trent, whereupon it departed at 11.55a.m. for Nottingham, arriving at 1.15p.m. Bourne, at 2.19p.m. and Melton Constable on the M.&G.N. section at 4p.m., were the next points of call and here the Sheringham and Cromer through coaches, were taken from the Manchester portion before the remaining section travelled on to arrive at Yarmouth (Beach) at 5.09p.m. Through coaches for Gorleston and Lowestoft (North) and Lowestoft (Central) were taken on over the Norfolk & Suffolk joint line (former M&GN & GER) arriving at 5.44p.m.

In the reverse direction Yarmouth, Melton Constable and Stoke-on-Trent were the points at which the various through sections were joined and separated, with a total time for the journey eleven minutes longer between Lowestoft and Liverpool — 10.30a.m. and 6p.m. respectively. This working in and out of Liverpool was normally the preserve of Midland engines, but in this 1924 view North Stafford 0-6-0 No. 67 pilots L&NWR 2-4-0 'Precedent' class No. 862 *Balmoral* on the Yarmouth to Liverpool working at Nottingham (Midland) Station, prior to a 3.21p.m. departure for Stoke.

V. Forster Collection

Plate 246: Compound No. 1157 pilots 'Patriot' No. 5514 *Holyhead* on the through line past Rugby in the 1930s.

G. Coltas

Plate 247: Midland 'Spinner' No. 644 pilots a Compound out of Derby for the south. The Birmingham and Bristol line leaves to the left of the picture. 'Spinners' were often used on the Midland line to St. Pancras as a pilot engine on the heaviest Midland trains.

W. L. Good

Plate 248: A brace of ex-Midland 2Ps. Nos. 520 and 525, in the early livery, with small Company initials, powering a 'down' Birmingham express out of Derby through Peartree and Normanton. The route directions on the Derby to Bristol line were 'down' to Bristol, 'up' to Derby, whereas elsewhere on the LMS, the 'down' line direction was away from London and towards London was 'up' — contrary to the layman's normal sense of direction.

D. J. White Collection

Plate 249: A light load of six carriages behind a powerful combinatin of 2-4-0 'Precedent' class No. 5011 *Director,* and an un-named Claughton 4-6-0 No. 5963. It may be a case of the pilot engine working back to its home shed, rather than take line occupancy as a separate light engine working.

Railways Yesteryear Collection

LMS FILMS

Plate 250: The LMS produced a range of films to publicise the Company and made these available to show around the system, where employees and their friends were invited to see them. They were popular and were soon made available for loan to other outside organisations, where it was hoped they would create increased interest in the Company, and would lead to additional traffic. This photograph shows some of the titles and addresses to which organisations could write.

Author's Collection

And now—the LMS in films

For loan and exhibition to Societies, Clubs, Schools, etc., the LMS Railway has available a new and extensive range of 16 mm. sub-standard films of travel and railway interest, embracing among other subjects :—

**BUILDING A PRINCESS ROYAL CLASS LOCOMOTIVE
CARRIAGE CONSTRUCTION • FREIGHT
PERMANENT WAY • SHIPS OF THE NARROW SEAS
PASSENGER TRAINS • ENGINE ON THE SHED**
and many scenic subjects

Applications and inquiries regarding these films, should be addressed to the
DISTRICT PASSENGER MANAGER, LMS RAILWAY:—
Euston Station, London — New Street Station, Birmingham
Hunt's Bank, Manchester — Lime Street Station, Liverpool
Barrow, Bristol, Chester, Derby, Leicester, Northampton, Sheffield, Stoke
COMMERCIAL MANAGER, Central Station, Glasgow

Printed in Great Britain by RICHARD TILLING, 106, Great Dover Street, London, S.E.1

Plate 251: The interior of No. 3 Film Unit vehicle, fitted out as a mobile cinema seating 52 persons in early 1938. As early as 1934 the LMS had converted a former L&NWR arc roof brake third vehicle for use as a film unit, a carrying vehicle equipped with the necessary projection equipment and staffed with two support staff. This toured the system and use was made of local halls to show films of a general nature, under a slogan 'See your own Railway on the Screen', where audiences of employees, relatives and friends and invited customers were encouraged to attend.

Some two years later a further coach conversion produced a cinema vehicle which could be used in the smaller towns and remoter parts of the system, and after the success of these tours, a third vehicle was added to the Unit — No. 3, shown here.

Wherever possible, staff were released to see the films in working hours but where this was not practical, they were invited to view in their own time. To ensure maximum attendance the units visited each centre on the same day or days of two consecutive weeks, so synchronising with different turns of duty.

Film titles included: 'Passenger Station Working'; 'Enemy No. 1' — The Rules & Regulations formed the basis of this film; 'Engine Shed'; 'Horse Grooming' and various titles on goods wagon and terminal operations. A number of other titles followed, and employees were invited to record their reactions to, and comments on, the films, and a summary of comments was printed in *On Time*, with payment made to the writer of each letter, or extract therefrom, which was used.

Author's Collection

PUSH-PULL

Plate 252: Push-pull trains were used in many locations on the LMS and they were a convenient way of providing a passenger service over a limited distance, in much the same way as the present day railcars are used. The need to move the locomotive from one end of a rake of carriages to the other was rendered unnecessary, and the time-factor saved was considerable. This view shows a 4-coach push-pull set with an ex-L&NWR driving trailer nearest the camera. Sandwiched between the stock is 2-4-2T No. 6653, pictured at Kenilworth in 1938, beside the tall home signal, also of former L&NWR origin. The two men are holding what appears to be a tape measure — modellers perhaps!

G. Coltas

Plate 253: Further detail for the modeller, with this view of the driving compartment interior of a former L&NWR push-pull trailer.

British Railways

FREIGHT BY ROAD

A great deal of merchandise was carried by LMS road vehicles, much of it to and from the railway goods yards as part of a combined road-rail journey. The Company also undertook road transportation on a throughout-basis, as a road transport operator in competition with many private hauliers. The Company owned a wide variety of road vehicle types including some heavy load types ideal for such operations. In this section examples of such traffic are shown.

Plate 254: Three vehicles loaded with Northrop Automatic Looms in cases ready to leave the manufacturers in Blackburn, en route to Spain, in 1933. The first and third vehicles are Karrier chassis, the other an AEC, all with bodies built at the Company's Wolverton Works.

National Railway Museum

Plate 255: An evening shift loading strawberries at Wisbech. In readiness for overnight despatch to markets around the country.

National Railway Museum

Plate 256: A Scammell tractor and trailer with solid tyres, with a bulky load ready for movement.

National Railway Museum

Plate 257: A Sentinel steam lorry and trailer with boiler casings.

STATIONERY BOILERS

There were almost 600 stationery boilers scattered around the system, and there were many different types for which detailed records were kept. All were subject to periodical inspection and certification. Many were used in the various works for heating during the winter period. A number of the LMS hotels had at least two which were in use continuously, and an even larger number were in use at the many pumping stations. The Company's laundries at Morecambe, Derby, and Hendon, and the Ale Stores beneath St. Pancras Station, and the Shoeburyness Well-Sinkers Department on the former London, Tilbury & Southend Railway were allocated a vertical boiler with cross water tubing, No. 177.

Included in the Stationary Boiler Records were those which were fitted in breakdown cranes, the Straker steam road lorry and a spare, and a number which, in 1929, were still in use as fire-engine boilers. A Foster steam tractor, based at Tamworth, was also included.

A number of withdrawn locomotives were used as stationary boilers to provide steam heating for passenger stock and both the Central and North stations at Blackpool were locations where these could be seen.

Plate 258: A Clarkson vertical boiler with Laidlaw Drew fittings.

Plate 259: A withdrawn Johnson Midland 1P 0-4-4 tank engine in use as a stationary boiler. Only the front pair of drivers from the original wheel set remain, and the bunker is resting on a small-wheeled truck. Modellers will note the coal neatly stacked to the left of the engine, a common feature at locomotive depots where coaling was done by hand..

Author's Collection

Plate 260: One of the stationary boiler installations at Blackpool (North) Station, a former L&YR 0-4-4T fitted with chimney extension, seen here in the early BR period.

G. Coltas

Plate 26l: The ornate chimney pots fitted to the Midland Grand Hotel, St. Pancras, with what appears to be cast plates numbered to correspond with the bedroom numbers.

J. Miller

THE CORONATION SCOT TRAIN . . . ARGUABLY THE COMPANY'S FINEST ACHIEVEMENT

Plate 262: A publicity picture at Euston using the specially-built 1939 train, rather than the train sets used in service from 1937. Note the flexible curtain between the carriages, and whilst the livery pattern was the same as the earlier stock, the livery was crimson lake with gold-edged black stripes running the length of the train.

British Railways

Plate 263: The 8-coach train is seen approaching Carpenders Park with the special 9.50a.m. Euston to Crewe (W700) working on 29th June 1937, whilst travelling at around 82m.p.h. Later on in the journey, after having passed Stafford, and when descending Madeley Bank on the section into Crewe, the train attained a maximum recorded speed of 114m.p.h., and this stood as the world record speed for steam locomotives. The locomotive is No. 6220 *Coronation*. The special was for the press, and aerial filming of the journey was carried out from the aeroplane seen above the train. Such was the speed as the train hurtled into Crewe, it is recorded that crockery in the kitchen cars was smashed and passengers were, to say the least, startled by the severe jolting as the train moved through crossovers.

Author's Collection

CARRY ON
LMS STAFF NEWS MAGAZINE

Vol. 8   DECEMBER 1947   No. 86

Princess Elizabeth as a child arriving at Glamis L.M.S. station on her way to visit her "Grannie" the Countess of Strathmore at Glamis Castle.
Escorting her is the late Glamis Station Master, Mr. Buchan.
See story on page 15.

Plate 264: The last LMS train to commence its journey, leaving St. Pancras at 11.50p.m. on 31st December 1947, headed by 'Jubilee' class 4-6-0 No. 5614 *Leeward Islands.*
British Railways

Plate 265: The final issue of the LMS staff News Magazine *Carry On* for the final month of LMS Railway operation. The young Princess Elizabeth is centre stage, seen arriving at Glamis Station on her way to Glamis Castle, the home of her 'Grannie' — the story refers to the holiday visits to the castle.

Author's Collection

LM&SR Y CO
BOUNDARY POST

INDEX TO LMS MISCELLANY VOL. 1

Plate Nos.

Exhibition Stands	1–2
Research Dept.	3–4
Railcars	5–9
Fire Trains Arrangements	10–14
Road Fire Vehicles	15–16
Road Transport Operations	
Horse Drawn Vehicles	17–21
Road Motors	22–23
Tramways	24–26
Motor Buses	27–29
Workshops	
Road Vehicle Dept.	30–33
Sewing Shop	34
Wagon and Van Construction	35
Cell, Timber and Lifting Shops	36–38
Locomotive Building and Repair	39–47
Tarpaulin Sheet Works	48–49
Sack Dept. — Clothing Factory	50–51
Concrete Depot	52
Electric Power Stations	53–54
Gas Works	55–56
Creosote Works	57–59
Permanent Way Activities	60–61
Civil Engineers Work	62
Winter Experiments	63
Ratcatchers	64
Brolly Turn	65
Locomotive Naming Ceremony	66–70
Barrows and Trolleys	71–79
Lifting Appliances	
Breakdown Cranes	80–84
Yard Cranes	85–89
Railway Air Services	90–95
Holidays — Caravans, Camping Coaches and Hotels	96–98
Canals	99–102
Steamer Services	103–105
Freight Handling	106–114
Passenger Stations	115–124, 126–128
Station Garden Competitions	125
Accidents	129–139
Wartime Destruction	140–142
Royal Travel	143–148
Pullman Cars	149–152
ARP and Ambulance Trains	153–158
Handbills	159
Shed Pass — MPDs	160–186
Traffic Scenes	187–211
Electrification	212–213
Water Troughs and Softening Plant	214–221
Wheel Tapper (Train Examiner)	222
Wagon Labels	223
First Aid	224–225
Publicity and Printed Material	226–238
The 'Coronation Scot'	239–242
Tickets	243
Luggage Labels	244
The LMS Beyond 1947	245–246

INDEX TO LMS MISCELLANY VOL. 2

Plate Nos.

LMS Employees	1–4
Collecting Dogs	5
Station Car Parking	6
Audit Office	7
Through Carriage Workings	8–9
Staff Accommodation and Amenities	10–12
Early Locomotive Liveries	13–14
First Diesel Express Service in Great Britain	15–18
Save to Travel Scheme	19
Holiday Contact Tickets	20–22
Excursion Traffic	23–31
Penny-a-mile and Land Cruises	32–33
LMS Operations in Ireland	34–49
Named Trains	50–51
Refreshment Rooms and Tea Rooms	52–53
Crockery	54–56
Cutlery	57–60
Glassware	61–63
Wear & Tear	64–65
Scrapyard	66–68
Docks, Harbours and Wharves	69–72
Dredging Plant	73–76
Derby Signal Works	77–82
Signalling	83–87
Fog and Snow Signalling Equipment	88–90
Wartime — The LMS War Effort:	
Employees	91–92
Evacuation of Children	93
Sandbag Protection	94
Armoured Trains	95
Military Training for Railwaymen	96–97
Mobile Canteens	98–99
Traffic	100
Salvage Campaign	101
Bomb Damage — Sheffield	102–103
Bomb Damage — St. Pancras	104–106
Ambulance Train	107
Aircraft Repairs by the LMS	108–111
BBC Broadcasts	112–113
Line Closure — Wick & Lybster Branch	114
Producer Gas	115
Indoor Air Raid Shelter	116
Victory Day — Euston Decorated	117
LMS Bric-a-Brac	118–128
Poster Publicity	129–134
Seat Reservations	135–137
Postcards	138–139
Parcel Stamps	140–142
Station Scenes	143–164
Telegraph and Telephone Communication	165–166
The Permanent Way	166–177
Chief Engineer's Department	178–187
Steam Turbine Locomotives	188–197
Basket Works and Basket Traffic	198–201
Registered Transit of Freight	202
Freight Traffic	203–215
Insurance of Livestock	216
Dyamometer Car Testing	217–218
LMS School of Transport	219–220
School of Signalling, Manchester	221
Turntables	222–225
Under Repair	226–229
Internal Works Transport	230–231
Engines and Carriages	232–243